Dale Evans Rogers

Dale Evans Rogers

Rainbow on a Hard Trail

Dale Evans Rogers
with Norman B. Rohrer

Foreword by Joni Eareckson Tada

Fleming H. Revell
A Division of Baker Book House Co
Grand Rapids, Michigan 49516

Published by Fleming H. Revell
a division of Baker Book House Company
P.O. Box 6287, Grand Rapids, MI 49516-6287

Paperback edition published 2000

Printed in the United States of America

Library of Congress Cataloging-in-Publication Data

Rogers, Dale Evans.
    Dale Evans Rogers : rainbow on a hard trail / Dale Evans Rogers with
Norman B. Rohrer ; foreword by Joni Eareckson Tada.
        p.   cm.
    Includes bibliographical references.
    ISBN 0-8007-1769-4 (cloth)
    ISBN 0-8007-5734-3 (paper)
    1. Rogers, Dale Evans. 2. Christian women—United States
Biography. I. Rohrer, Norman B. II. Title.
BR1725.R63A3   1999
277.3'082'092—dc21
[b]   99-22391

For current information about all releases from Baker Book House, visit our web site:
http://www.bakerbooks.com

In memory of Roy,
and fifty years of happy trails
together

Contents

Foreword

Some childish things are supposed to be put away as we grow older. Like the Roy Rogers lunch box from Mrs. Collins' first-grade class in 1955. Remember yours? (It was shaped like a chuck wagon, with branding-iron burns on the sides.) Somewhere in the basement of our old house is a chest containing LPs from Roy Rogers and the Sons of the Pioneers, a sheriff's badge, a cap-gun-and-holster set, and at least twenty-five tattered comic books showcasing Trigger, Bullet, Nellie Belle, and the rest of the crew on the Rogers' ranch. These are a few things from my childhood I've "put away."

Yet some remembrances I can't shelve. I treasure every card I receive from Dale Evans Rogers, as if the name itself were an icon. At the side of my computer, I keep a couple of snapshots of Dale and me when we spoke together at a banquet near Santa Barbara.

And in our home is a framed and autographed picture of Roy and Dale on their horses.

Why do I keep these items in sight and within reach?

They inspire. They refresh. They remind me of the importance of example. Each provides a strong link between the past and the present, highlighting the promise that "in due season we shall reap, if we faint not" (Gal. 6:9).

It's that way whenever I'm around Dale. She inspires and refreshes. She reminds me of the importance of serving as an example. Not as a celebrity but as a person who has held on to the grace of God through every heartache and hardship. I thought of this the last time I parked my wheelchair next to Dale's. Sitting in our chairs, we're about the same height. We joked about how we once sat in our saddles (yes, I used to ride horses, too), and we kibitzed about flat tires and neck aches from looking up at others.

We also talked about our mutual love for the Lord Jesus, our dogged persistence in facing trials head-on, and our lively hope of heaven. "Oh, honey," she said to me, "I just loved that book you wrote on heaven." Knowing Dale, I'm sure she meant it.

This is what impresses me most. She *means* her faith. Dale Evans Rogers doesn't speak from scripts when it comes to Christ. She speaks from the heart. She doesn't need a teleprompter. The Spirit does the prompting. She never comes across rehearsed—her words and witness are as fresh as the grace that turns every bruising into a blessing.

This is what will strike you about this book. From the first chapter to the last, your heart will be moved as you read how Dale has dealt with her recent physical setbacks. You'll learn of a woman whose soul is settled and whose peace is profound. You'll discover someone who leads not with parade and noise but by influence. And like me, you will think, If this woman in her eighties, with all her aches and pains, can do it, I can, too.

Thank you, Dale, for going out ahead and charting the wilderness. Thank you for blazing a footpath for people like me who struggle with affliction and heartache. Bless you for teaching us that the hope of heaven is just beyond trail's end. And may God shine his favor on you for showing us that the Lord Jesus lights our path every step of the way.

Come to think of it, this book is just the trail guide we need.

—Joni Eareckson Tada

Acknowledgments

With Affection and Thanks

For my wonderful children, who supported me throughout my harrowing experiences: Tom, Cheryl, Linda, Dusty, Marion, and Dodie; for my fourteen grandchildren; for my thirty-three great-grandchildren; and for my sons- and daughters-in-law—especially for Larry Barnett, who prodded me to record these blessed godsends during my recuperation.

To my physician, Dr. Dale Isaeff; to my surgeons, Dr. Jeffrey Ballard and Dr. J. David Killeen at the Loma Linda University Medical Center; to Dr. John Chen and his healing art of acupuncture; to my pastor, William Hansen, for his shepherd's care; to Joni Eareckson Tada, my sister in suffering, who graciously wrote the foreword; and especially to my faithful home-care provider Martha Brown, who exemplifies biblical love by selflessly attending to all my needs.

And in Loving Memory Of

Roy Rogers, "King of the Cowboys," a servant of Christ without guile and my loving husband for nearly fifty-one years, who departed to be with Christ as this book was being written.

If my story of the devastation of a stroke and recovery under the healing hand of God can help spread love's message as the Master taught, my suffering will not be in vain. Indeed, serving others for Christ's sake is the rainbow on a hard trail.

1

Unhappy Trails

Peace is not the absence of trouble, but the presence of God.

J. Oswald Chambers

While sorting my mail one day, I came across a letter from a young fan in Korea who ended her note with these affirming words: "You must be having a wonderful time, enjoying your healthy body."

I leaned back on our sofa and smiled. A healthy body. Yes, a gift from God. The year was 1992; I would be eighty years old on Halloween. Having lived through the deaths of three of our nine children and through the trials of Roy's surgical procedures to remedy pain from years of rough riding and movie stunts, I felt invincible. We were supremely happy in our home at Apple Valley, California, surrounded by most of our children and enjoying a constant flow of friendly visitors from all over the world to the nearby Roy Rogers and Dale Evans Museum in Victorville.

Behind us forever were the frantic days of movie-making in Hollywood, the City of Dreams. To us who lived there, it was more often eating cold meals on the run, shooting dangerous scenes, acting creatively when you least felt like it, enduring sleepless nights and weeks of family separations, memorizing many pages of script. God was good to bless me with a strong constitution.

Into the Refiner's Fire

In anticipation of Mother's Day 1992, I made certain that no obligations would take me out of town, so I could be with our children. But in the night season before the sun rose on the big day of my sixty-fourth celebration as a mother, I was in trouble. For dinner that evening I had prepared some fruit for dessert but had no appetite to enjoy it. I slipped off to bed, deciding to get a good night's rest to be ready for the arrival of our children and grandchildren on Mother's Day.

Soon after midnight I was awakened by horrible pain shooting from my heart up into my neck and ears—pain so intense I could only gasp in whispers for help. Roy called 911 and soon the red lights of an ambulance were flashing in our driveway out front. The medics gave me a shot to deaden the pain as I was sped toward St. Marys Regional Medical Center in Apple Valley.

Lord, I prayed silently, *did it hurt like this when you died for me on the cross? And you had* nothing *to deaden the pain, nor did you deserve your suffering.* Over and over I prayed as we sped along, *Abide with me . . . please . . . abide with me.* As the pain increased I pleaded, *Are you there, Lord? I cannot take it much longer. I'm ready. Take me home.*

By that time the ambulance had arrived at the emergency entrance, where a nurse administered an injection so that I quickly lost consciousness. What sweet relief the Lord ordains for the suffering. By morning my lungs had filled up so much I could not breathe. Tests showed that a valve in my heart had been badly damaged, allowing blood to flow into my lungs. A bold incision and the implanting of a steel ring stopped the valve from malfunctioning. My heart was stabilized and my lungs began to clear.

Throughout this unexpected refining, I learned to escape to the quiet center of my being. There I simply wait upon the Lord, trusting him to work out events through his faultless timing. The healthy body to which the Korean girl had referred in her letter was wearing out.

Have you endured the Refiner's fire? I learned, as did the apostle Paul, that "there hath no temptation taken you but such as is common to man: but God is faithful, who will not suffer you to be tempted above that ye are able; but will with the temptation also make a way to escape" (1 Cor. 10:13).

God's Word is true. With his help I was able to bear my trial. Gradually my heart grew stronger, its beat steadied by a battery-powered pacemaker surgically inserted just under the skin, with a wire running into my heart. I was certain that I would never suffer another Mother's Day like that one. But our ways are not God's. He had further disciplines for me.

Another Day in May

Four years after my heart attack, preparation for Mother's Day 1996 began early. The chance of suffering another medical crisis on my special day seemed remote. Only happy days lay ahead as far as I could see. Roy had survived triple-bypass heart surgery, corrective back and neck surgeries, painful surgery on a large aneurysm on his aorta, and pneumonia.

Now we were finally enjoying our sunset years in peace, eager once again to receive our extended family in our big house at the edge of a golf course in Apple Valley. My son and his family would be coming from Sacramento, where Tom serves as minister of music. Cheryl, Dusty, Marion, Dodie, and their families lived close by and would be joining us with their children. Linda Lou and her family would be coming from central California. What wonderful kids, and what winsome grandchildren! The day would be perfect.

My Mother's Day of 1992, spent in searing pain inside drab hospital walls, was now a distant memory. Thank God my heart attack was behind me for good.

Of course, empty chairs around the table still brought pain to our hearts. Our children who wouldn't be with us this Mother's Day of 1996 were not forgotten. Robin's death left a big hole in my heart. Through my book *Angel Unaware,* the Lord gave me an extraordinary opportunity to tell of his sustaining grace during times of great trial. Without his grace my book would have been just another testimonial from an entertainer. By sharing our experiences with Robin publicly, I was able to help get Down's syndrome children out of the closet, to encourage their parents to seek the help they needed, and to see other handicapped children receive love, concern, and assistance instead of frowns of embarrassment.

When our Debbie was killed in a church bus accident on the San Diego Freeway while on a mission to help poor people in Mexico, our shock and intense grief were overwhelming. My suffering was so unnerving that I doubted God's goodness for a brief period. Roy, as well, struggled with what he considered to be a senseless death. But again the Lord opened through all this the door to a new level of witness—this time to parents who had lost children suddenly in a similar way.

Sandy's death in Germany while serving with the U.S. Army could have devastated us, needless as it was. But God had prepared us for this refinement by having Sandy write us a letter that we received a week before his death. In it he expressed his commitment to the Savior and his desire to establish a Christian home with the young woman to whom he was engaged. His death became another reminder of our total dependence upon God for life and breath—and upon his sustaining presence in the midst of a trial.

God's refining fire was put to my pride the year I was chosen Mother of the Year and then removed after the annual convention in New York, when the committee learned about my failed marriages before I gave my life to Christ. Sponsors of the event kindly explained that no woman who had been divorced could be nominated Mother of the Year. While it was a humbling experience, I was grateful that the committee had acted immediately, because they were right and proper in what they did. Our country desperately needs exemplary parents and stable homes. I won't even accept a position as deaconess in the church because of my youthful divorces. That doesn't stop my witness to the power of Jesus Christ to transform lives. Perhaps it increases the impact of responsible acts; as Luke 12:48 points out, "unto whomsoever much is given, of him shall be much required."

Soon after I wrote *Angel Unaware,* Art Linkletter asked me to be a guest on his television program. The purpose was to talk about the book, for it was making quite a splash. On the program, Art asked me, "What made you write this book?" So I took the opportunity to tell him and the audience about giving my life to Christ, about how his presence had sustained me during the trauma of losing Robin after having her with us for two years. Then I shared with Art's audience how God had held me up after her death. Art was surprised because he had not expected me to make such a clear witness of my faith.

Since experiencing trials in his own family, Art has supported Christian efforts to deal with drugs and other problems that are tearing at the fabric of our society. However, he no longer has his own program. It's strange how show business will finally ease you out once you fall in love with Jesus Christ.

Harbingers

A few weeks before Mother's Day 1996, toward which I looked with eager anticipation, I noticed a strange feeling in my left arm. At first it was only an annoying little twitch of nerves as my arm fell limp at my side. My children noticed but I assured them my arm had merely fallen asleep. Surely blood would flow again and it would be as good as new. This numbness occurred several times but I ignored it. I didn't want to spoil another Mother's Day celebration as my heart attack had done four years earlier.

Several weeks passed but the occasional numbness did not. Friends persuaded me to ask my doctor to have a look. Afraid that I would spoil the family activities for this Mother's Day celebration, I put off an appointment for several weeks. Finally, early in May I took my family's advice and scheduled an appointment. Dr. Dale Isaeff at the Loma Linda University Medical Center identified my troubles as Transient Ischemic Attacks—a phenomenon caused by a clump of blood cells blocking off a main neck artery carrying blood to the brain. "These are usually temporary," he said, "because the clump is soon broken up and swept away, restoring blood flow."

There being no immediate danger, I bravely rode from the doctor's office near San Bernardino to Trinity Broadcasting Network's studios in Santa Ana, California, for my television show, *A Date with Dale*, which I have hosted for a number of years. I seemed to have my old vigor back. There was a new song of gratitude in my heart. The world looked bright and God's promises were more precious than ever.

In the home of our son Dusty during a party for employees at the Roy Rogers and Dale Evans Museum, I noticed a slurring in my speech. I began pronouncing the names of good friends in funny ways. What meant this odd behavior? To my great relief, all confusion had disappeared by morning. I thought again, with mistaken zeal, *I'm free!*

My Mother's Day celebration was only a week away when another unwelcomed Trans Ischemic Attack left its calling card. I had fallen asleep on the couch in our den while watching television. Roy went to bed without disturbing me. When I awoke, I knew something was terribly wrong with my body. I struggled to raise myself to a sitting position, but there was no strength in my left arm.

"Roy!" I called out desperately.

But my husband, who was hard of hearing as a result of all those movie gunfights, had removed his hearing aids before going to bed and couldn't hear my call.

"Lord," I whispered, panic rising in my throat, "please help me."

I continued to struggle, finally getting myself upright on the sofa. With the help of a cane, I found my balance and staggered slowly to the bedroom, where I fell across our bed like a lump of clay, fully clothed. There I drifted into fitful sleep and yielded to dreams of years gone by.

2

Woman in a Hurry

While we were yet sinners, Christ died for us.
Romans 5:8

My dreams that night carried me back to the slow and easy world of Uvalde, Texas. On October 31, 1912, in the midst of Halloween revelry, the small town's population swelled by one new citizen—me, Frances Octavia Smith. My parents lived on a farm owned by my grandfather, near Italy, Texas, and I relished the attention the eldest child receives from doting parents and six aunts. In my self-centeredness I considered the arrival of baby brother Hillman to be an unwelcome intrusion. With loud crying and tears I let it be known to all that the Smith domain was not big enough for the two of us. But that immature selfishness soon passed. Despite my initial petty outbursts, Hillman and I became inseparable chums and faced the world as a team.

At the age of ten I knelt at the altar of a little Baptist church in Osceola, Arkansas, in my Sunday-go-to-meeting dress, to make Jesus Christ Lord of my life. Unfortunately, the lure of worldly pleasures caused this headstrong, ambitious girl to stray far from his teachings. I relished many vain pursuits during the Depression years of the early thirties and drank deeply from polluted springs.

Time sped by in a blur, but not fast enough for this young singer. At fourteen I eloped with my high school sweetheart, a young man only eighteen years old. After a year of wandering and the birth of our son, Tom, we were separated permanently by divorce.

First Steps to Stardom

As a single parent, I pursued a career in music, which I've always loved, and landed a job with local radio stations WMC and WREC in Memphis, singing and playing the piano.

During my time as a staff singer at radio station WHAS in Louisville, Kentucky, I changed my married name, Frances Fox, to the *nom de song* Marian Lee. Joe Eaton, WHAS station manager, thought that name was trite and trendy, so he informed me that my name would thereafter be Dale Evans.

"That's a boy's name!" I indignantly informed him, but Joe wouldn't budge. He told me of a beautiful actress in the era of silent films whose name was Dale Winter. He wanted me to be Dale in honor of her. The surname Evans was added simply because Joe decided it was euphonious. It could roll easily off the lips of radio announcers.

My career in music was sporadic, so I enrolled in a Memphis business college to become a secretary, just in case I needed to keep body and soul together with a nine-to-five job. But a love of music prevailed and I found the typewriter tedious.

One day I sat at my desk in the insurance office, staring vaguely at an accident claim form in my typewriter. I was trying to think up words to fit a tune I had just composed, when the boss walked in. He stood there looking at me for a moment, and then he exploded. "Young lady, I think you are in the wrong business!"

My fingers flew to the typewriter keyboard, and I typed like a maniac. He walked away, turned, came back to me, and said, "How would you like to sing on a radio program?" The heavens opened. Bells rang and trumpets sounded. *Would* I? He asked me if I could accompany myself on the piano; if I could, he might just get me on the radio as a guest on a program in which he had a sponsor's interest.

The next Friday night, Dale Evans made her radio debut, playing and singing "Mighty Lak a Rose." In those days, you were permitted to dedicate your song to anyone you chose, so my first dedication—the first of many to come—was to my son, Tommy. Someone must have liked my performance, for I was offered a regular spot at the radio station.

I held on to the secretarial job because radio offered only experience, no pay. But how I loved performing! Civic organizations in town began inviting me to sing at luncheons and banquets. Once in a while I got paid for these appearances in real money (as much as twenty dollars); mostly I was paid in chicken croquettes and peas. But the experience was invaluable. I learned to meet and face the public, and within a few months I had moved up from that first small radio station to the most powerful station in Memphis.

When the big dance bands came to town, I would go with an escort to hear them, and sometimes I would be asked to sing a number with the orchestra, using a big, old-fashioned megaphone. My name began to rise in popular demand. I reasoned that if I could crack Memphis, I could crack Chicago, and soon I was off to conquer the Windy City.

I became the featured soloist in such notable hotels as the Blackstone (Balinese Room); the Sherman (Panther Room), singing with jazz legend Fats Waller; the Drake (Camellia Room); and the Chez Paree Supper Club. Anson Weeks hired me as a vocalist for his orchestra just as they began a major tour to the West Coast. To stay on the team, I was forced to place my young son, Tom, with Grandma Smith on our Texas farm, which he loved.

Hollywood!

Out of the blue one afternoon in 1940, I received a telegram from an agent in Hollywood who had heard me sing on a broadcast that reached California. He asked for photographs. If he liked them, he would arrange a screen test.

I laughed as I read the telegram. I had no desire whatever to go to Hollywood. I was aiming at stardom in Broadway musical comedies. Besides, I did not think I was pretty enough to be in pictures. What's more, I wasn't an actress—and I was twenty-eight years old. So I ignored the telegrams as they came—one after another. Finally I showed them to my program director. "Give it a whirl, Dale," he suggested.

Give it a whirl? Still laughing and still unable to believe the invitation, I had the assigned glamour photos taken, and sent the best of the batch to the agent, Joe Rivkin.

"Take a plane immediately for a screen test at Paramount Studios," read the next wire.

My heart was pounding as I boarded a sleeper plane for Hollywood from Chicago. This was my first flight of such a long distance. I had never before crossed the fruited plain in a passenger aircraft. Ten feet off the ground, on our way to cruising altitude, I developed a severe earache and suffered with it all night long. In those days airplanes had no pressurized cabins to compensate for high altitudes. A flight attendant dropped warm oil into my ears. Nothing helped. I slept not a wink and could eat no breakfast because of nausea. What a way to show up for an audition.

As the plane started its descent for landing in Burbank, I wished with all my heart that I could have been anywhere but there. I wished I had never heard of a Hollywood agent, wished I had remained in Chicago. But of course I had to meet him. *Lucky for me,* I thought, *I can wear dark glasses to hide the ravages of the painful night.*

I glanced out the window of the airplane and saw a thin man pacing up and down on the tarmac. That had to be him. I'd read in a book that all agents are nervous and high-strung.

Somehow I got down those steps to the ground and found courage enough to walk toward the stranger and ask, "Are you Joe Rivkin?"

The man stopped pacing and stared at me with an incredulous look on his face. "Oh no!" he exclaimed. "Are you Dale Evans?"

"Oh, Mr. Rivkin," I said, "I had a terrible night."

He seemed not to hear me, just kept staring. Suddenly he barked, "Take off those glasses."

I pulled them off as slowly as possible. He caught his breath and turned pale. Finally he mumbled, "Well, you certainly don't look like your pictures." I wanted to run back into the plane and take off for anywhere in the world but Hollywood. What a welcome!

He collected my baggage and threw it into the trunk of his car. As we started down the road for Hollywood, he looked down, spotted the wedding ring on my finger, and howled, "You didn't tell me you were married!"

"You didn't ask me."

A long, painful silence prevailed as the car made its way along a broad concrete thoroughfare lined with palm trees.

"How old are you?"

I had been told to say I was twenty-two, so that's what I told Joe.

"No," he cut in, "you are twenty-one. Got it? And you are *single*. Understand?"

I understood and I didn't like it. I resented the whole setup. Didn't even answer him. Inside my head I was making plans. I decided to go through the entire screen test, enjoy a California vacation, see Hollywood, and then get back to Chicago as fast as I could to resume my musical career.

Joe Rivkin drove as though he wasn't interested in getting anywhere fast. From time to time he looked me over, growing more disgusted with each look.

"I don't like your lipstick," he said. "Don't wear it anymore. And I don't like your hair either. We'll have to do something about it."

We drove up in front of the Hollywood Plaza Hotel, where Joe parked the car quickly and rushed me downstairs to the beauty salon. "See what you can do with her," he told the operator. "And step on it. We have to be at Paramount in an hour."

I felt like a prize pig being groomed for exhibition at a small-town fair. Suddenly I didn't care what might happen at Paramount. All I wanted was a little rest.

The beautician gave me a stinging facial massage. ("Get a little blood in her face," Rivkin had told her.) The girl tinted my light brown hair with an auburn rinse and sent me off to dress for a luncheon with Mr. Meiklejohn, a casting director at Paramount.

In Chicago a dark dress with furs and gloves was the proper attire, so I put on a sheer dark dress, selected a fur (my only fur), pulled on a pair of spotless white gloves, and walked into the lobby with all the pride and confidence of Cleopatra on her barge. Rivkin saw me coming and put his hands over his eyes.

"Who's dead?" he asked. "What's with the black dress?"

I could have popped him but I kept control of my temper. À la Cleopatra I replied haughtily, "In Chicago, sir, this is proper dress for a business meeting at noon."

"Well, you're not in Chicago now. You're in Hollywood, and in Hollywood you wear bright colors, with flowers—casual. But it's too late now. Come on!" By the time we reached the office of the casting director, I was shaking like a leaf, inside and outside.

Mr. Meiklejohn was gentle and kind as we smiled at each other and shook hands. He said, "Dale, you remind me a lot of my wife when she first came to Hollywood." I liked that and I liked him. He took my arm and led me through a maze of people in the dining room; they all stopped eating and craned their necks to see "the new one." I wished the floor would open up and swallow me. At the table, I felt like a tennis ball in a fast game.

"Dale," Mr. Meiklejohn asked, "how old are you?"

"Twenty-one," shouted Joe Rivkin.

The director looked long and hard at my face, and then he said, "I'm a little worried about the nose. A trifle too long for the chin." I felt like telling him that the good Lord had given me the nose, and if he didn't mind, I'd keep it, but I never had a chance to say anything. Rivkin beat me to it with, "Don't worry about the nose; we'll have some of it taken off."

Mr. Meiklejohn: "Dale, do you dance?"

Mr. Rivkin: "Dance? She makes Eleanor Powell look like a bum."

Miss Evans: "No, Mr. Meiklejohn, I can't dance. I can't even do a time step." I explained that I had turned down a chance at a part in the stage musical *Hold onto Your Hats* because I was not a professional dancer. I could do ballroom well enough, but not solo.

Bill Meiklejohn almost blew his top when he heard that. He gave Joe Rivkin the kind of icy stare that would have frozen a polar bear into silence. But Joe wasn't frozen; he promised quickly and glibly that I could pick up the dancing in no time at all.

The director explained that I had been summoned for a screen test with an eye to the ingenue lead in the picture *Holiday Inn,* starring Bing Crosby and Fred Astair. They were looking for a new female personality for the picture, but since I could not dance, I couldn't fit the part; however, they would make a screen test anyway. Perhaps something might come of it.

The lunch ended quickly, and I was taken to the wardrobe department and introduced to Miss Edith Head, who fitted me out with a dress and a fur muff formerly worn by Barbara Stanwyck.

Then the drama coach took me under his wing. He picked a scene from Marlene Dietrich's picture *Blue Angel* and told me that MacDonald Carey was to play opposite me.

I worked hard all that week and the next. Joe Rivkin watched me as a hawk watches a chicken. He saw to it that I did not stay out late and that I had plenty of time to study my part in the test. He also told me what I could and could not eat, in the interest of reducing my weight. I grew more and more apprehensive about deceiving the studio about my age and about the fact that I had a son.

Finally I could stand it no longer. I walked up to Joe Rivkin and told him that I had to talk to him right now before things went any further. We slipped out into the alley behind the studio. I turned and faced him like a cornered criminal and blurted out, "Mr. Rivkin, I have not been completely honest with you, and I can't go on with this thing until you know the facts. I am not twenty-one; I am twenty-eight. I have a son who is twelve years old. He lives with me."

Joe immediately had the solution: "You will have to send him away to school."

That made my situation worse. I refused, saying that if Tom could not come to Hollywood with me, we would stay in Chicago.

Rivkin tried another tack: "Tom is your brother. Do you understand?"

I still didn't like it, but at least this ruse gave me the chance to have Tom with me in Hollywood, and that was something. So I said, "It's all right with me if it's all right with Tom."

It was all right with Tom. He commented, "It sounds pretty silly, but you can do anything you want, Mother, as long as I myself don't have to lie." I figured that with what I could make on a good Hollywood job, I could send him to college and give him the musical education he so desperately wanted. But I was certain nothing would come of the screen test anyway, so why worry?

I took the test, then flew home to Chicago to wait it out. Actually, I was still hankering for a place not in the movies but in a New York stage show, so I didn't worry too much about Joe Rivkin and Hollywood. I had almost put Hollywood out of my mind when I got a call from Mr. Rivkin. He told me excitedly that while Paramount had not taken up their option on me, Twentieth Century Fox had inked me at a salary of four hundred dollars per week on a one-year contract.

That was a lot of money in 1940. Tom and I talked it over and over and over. I decided to give it a whirl. For this initial move I received small parts in two pictures—*Orchestra Wives* and *Girl Trouble*. After that I signed with the top-ranked *Chase and Sanborn Show,* which was broadcast nationwide. I became a featured regular with Don Ameche, Jimmy Durante, Edgar Bergen, and Charlie McCarthy.

Herbert J. Yates, head of Republic Studios, took notice of me in these roles. He signed me to a one-picture contract for *Swing Your Partner,* which gave him a one-year option. The option was later exercised, so I was cast in several contemporary movies, including a John Wayne western in which I was a featured singer.

Paradise Regained

In the early forties Herb Yates was inspired by the successful stage play *Oklahoma.* He decided to expand the female lead in westerns and to adopt this format for one of his biggest stars, Roy Rogers. Herb reasoned that his "little gal from Texas" had a large following by then and a growing reputation as a singer. And being from Texas, she could surely ride 'n' rope 'em as required. The former proved to be correct but the latter had been somewhat exaggerated. Nevertheless, history was made and destiny fulfilled in 1944 with the release of *The Cowboy and the Senorita*—the first of twenty-eight films Roy and I would make together. This on-screen team became an off-screen team as well on New Year's Eve 1947. Roy and I walked down the aisle to be married at the Flying L Ranch in Davis, Oklahoma, where we had just completed filming *Home in Oklahoma*. When the owner of the ranch learned we were to be married, he offered his ranch as a wedding site.

Ours became an instant family, including my son Tom, Roy's adopted daughter Cheryl, along with Linda Lou and Roy Rogers Jr. ("Dusty"), both of whom were born to Roy's first wife, Grace Arline Wilkins Rogers, who died of a blood clot a few days after Dusty's birth in November 1946. Later came our own little Robin Elizabeth, who lived two years and then died of brain fever caused by mumps. Our family increased with the adoption of Merry Little Doe ("Dodie"), a full-blooded Choctaw Indian—an adoption allowed only because Roy was part Choctaw; John David ("Sandy"), an abused and battered little boy from an orphanage in Kentucky; Marion ("Mimi"), our foster child from Scotland; and finally Debbie Lee from Korea (whose father was a GI of Puerto Rican ancestry).

The story of my marriage to Roy Rogers, our commitment to the Lord Jesus Christ, our lives on the silver screen, our performances in rodeos all over this country, our appearances on the platform with Billy Graham at some of his crusades, our nine children, the building of the Roy Rogers and Dale Evans Museum in Victorville, California—it all seems now like a dream.

At the Gate of Life City

Suddenly I awoke at our home in Apple Valley, still fully dressed and still lying in rumpled clothes on the bed where I had fallen the night before. I feebly looked around our bedroom. Roy was still deep in slumber. Brilliant hues from a California sunrise in the high desert were lighting up the dawn, illuminating the draperies on the east window. I took stock of my desperate situation. *Lord,* I prayed, *I belong to you. I am in your hands. Show me what to do now.*

God's provision was home-care provider Martha Brown. She packed me into a wheelchair, rolled me to our van, and drove me to nearby St. Marys Regional Medical Center for diagnosis.

A brain scan and an artery test showed that I had 90 percent blockage in the right carotid artery. I was referred to the Loma Linda University Medical Center, where physicians strongly recommended corrective surgery—immediately. Was I strong enough, at eighty-three, to endure the procedure? Could my weak heart stand the strain? It was time to commit the matter to the Lord in prayer. He had never failed to answer my supplications. And so, recognizing his sovereign love, I conceded that Mother's Day celebrations would once again have to be postponed.

3

Some through the Fire

The great Physician now is near,
The sympathizing Jesus;
He speaks, the drooping heart to cheer,
Oh, hear the voice of Jesus.

William Hunter

How strange it all seemed. One week I was happily planning a Mother's Day party, tending to the needs of my family, singing on television, writing letters, making speeches, and the next I was lying helpless on a bed of pain, listening apprehensively as a physician outlined the surgery designed to cure the effects of a stroke. I was eighty-three, the same age at which my mother had died. Would I be privileged to live longer than she?

Strokes occur when brain tissue dies, either from a lack of blood supply or from bleeding into the tissues (cerebral hemorrhage). The carotid artery on the right side of my neck, carrying blood to my brain, had become completely blocked. That explained the paralysis in my left arm. Warnings had been surfacing for months: mild numbness, then inconvenience, then slurred speech—who knows where it would have ended? Now I stood to be sidelined permanently, perhaps slain, by the clogging of the artery to the brain. Impending possibilities were blindness, loss of speech, hearing loss, difficulty in swallowing, vertigo, complete paralysis—the end of a fulfilling life. In prayer and with trust in the mercy and grace of my heavenly Father, I was able confidently to place myself in the hands of experienced Christian physicians at the prestigious Loma Linda University Medical Center, built and operated by Christians of the Seventh-day Adventist Church. But there was an ache in my party-loving heart because I was missing out on a lot of fun at home.

Our staff at the Roy Rogers and Dale Evans Museum had set May 18, 1996, as the date for an evening of celebration called "Under Western Stars." It was to be our very first benefit to help the museum financially. The museum event was scheduled to raise funds for repairs and remodeling. A splendid dinner with entertainment and auctions of donated memorabilia marked an event I longed to attend. I had begged my physicians to postpone surgery so I could participate in the program, but they would not budge.

So while friends and fans began to gather for our big party in the museum complex, while guitars would be strummed and favorite songs sung, I was being prepped for surgery to be performed when the sun came up. My disappointment was keen, but I could sing the old Salvation Army hymn:

> Faith, mighty faith, the promise sees
> and looks to God above.
> Laughs at impossibilities and cries,
> "It shall be done!"

Under the Knife

On the morning of May 17, 1996, with Roy and our children gathered at my bedside for prayer, we asked God to take the surgeon's hands in his and to guide the knife so the operation could be completed successfully. My family was warned that my recovery would be slow and painful, particularly when feeling returned to my left shoulder and left leg. Had I known what lay ahead, I would not have felt prepared to face my armageddon.

By nightfall on the day of surgery, after the procedure was done, the drugged sleep of anesthesia gradually wore off and numbness lost its grip on my body. In its place came searing pain and nervous apprehension. The predicted depression struck me hard. I was wheeled on the operating table back to my hospital room, where family members had strict orders to give me plenty of rest during recuperation. I definitely did not want to hear what Dr. Dale Isaeff told me: "Because of your age, your recovery will be long."

All wired up to monitors, I began to thrash back and forth on my bed, convinced I would soon be leaving this vale of tears. "O Lord," I mumbled, quoting a hymn, "abide with me . . . abide with me."

As it had since God created the world, the sun rose on May 18, the day after surgery. I was not a peaceful patient. I tossed and turned nervously, convinced I was permanently disabled. Roy was alone when the phone rang at 10:30 P.M. A newspaper reporter had heard that I had died during surgery at Loma Linda, and was phoning for confirmation. "Is it true?" he asked Roy.

God was good to keep Roy from suffering a stroke himself at that shocking news. My husband assured the reporter that I was still alive, though not yet well, on planet earth.

For a type A personality like mine, news that my recovery would be lengthy was a crushing blow. Our pastor, the Reverend O. William Hansen, of the Church of the Valley Presbyterian, reminded me that God knows what to allow each one of his children to experience and that "all things work together for good to those who love God, to those who are the called according to His purpose" (Rom. 8:28 NKJV). After all, there is "a time to be born, and a time to die," according to Ecclesiastes 3:1–8, "a time to weep, and a time to laugh." My laughing was over for a time. All I felt like doing was mourning.

On the day following my operation, I fell asleep at approximately 4:30 P.M. When I awoke, my room was dark and I was confused. Was it morning or evening? I could see headlights from automobiles on the San Bernardino Freeway zipping by in the distance. I looked at the clock on the wall of my room: 9:15. I rang for my nurse.

"It's still evening," she told me.

This news left me quite disoriented for some reason, feeling alone and in a mild panic. My reeling mind told me that the world had come to an end and that I was lying in Loma Linda University Medical Center helpless and alone. With tears in my eyes I cried, "Help,

Lord!" And with the weight of the world on my wobbly shoulders, I closed my eyes again to sleep.

From the Clipboard

Dr. Jeffrey Ballard, a vascular surgeon on the team at Loma Linda, had ascertained upon examination that I was on my way to having a major stroke "right before our eyes."

"That made our patient's condition quite disturbing," he said in his report to my family. In his typically thorough and deliberate manner, he went on to explain in lay terms the selected procedure. "We used a technique in the operating room that was quite effective," he explained. "We used a shunt to bypass the area so that blood would flow to the brain during the operation. When a patient has carotid [blocked] symptoms, it always looks as though a bomb went off in the artery. There is usually a lot of diseased plaque that's very friable [easily reduced to powder]. Sometimes you get bleeding into that plaque.

"The bottom line is that things were flicking off there and 'going north' to cause problems. What happens is that you get embolization of debris, and that goes into the brain and then into the very small arteries. That area, then, doesn't get blood supply. But it's not a 'global' lack of blood supply from the neck arteries. Things are 'going north' from that area to become trapped in the small arteries of the brain. And that is what was happening to Mrs. Rogers. And it was happening repeatedly. We had to be extremely careful in the operating room to make sure that we didn't cause something to dislodge. That could have been a major problem."

Dr. Ballard propped open the carotid artery with a little patch of dacron. His procedure reduced stenosis (narrowing of a blood vessel). The patch made the vessel a bit larger. My surgeon also fashioned a nice, smooth flow-surface so nothing would flick off later and go up into my brain.

Dr. Ballard further explained in his report, "In the operating room, I put the ultrasound machine right back on the artery before I left. We didn't want to have any technical defects. When everything looks great, we close everything, and another ultrasound is obtained about six months later. In Mrs. Rogers' case, the follow-up ultrasound showed that there was minimal damage. Everything looked great.

"She was a very high-risk patient," he continued. "I could have fallen flat on my face with that decision to operate. Believe me, when you're kind of a young surgeon and you're operating on Dale Evans Rogers at Loma Linda University Medical Center, the last thing you want to have is a problem."

Dr. Ballard discussed the case with his associate, Dr. J. David Killeen, and my physician, Dr. Dale Isaeff, both vascular specialists.

"Obviously the timing was perfect," said Dr. Ballard, "because she did very well. We were taught here at Loma Linda how to do endarterectomy very well, and our overall risk of stroke for the entire vascular surgery section is very low. It's a rare patient that has a problem with carotid surgery here."

The goal of my surgery was not primarily to get me back to normal (which was impossible) but to prevent a major addition to the present problem and to prevent a major debilitating stroke in the future. If I had suffered a stroke during surgery, according to the surgeons, I would have been a quadriplegic and could not have moved anything at all. My surgeons remarked about the faithful attendance of my loving family at the hospital. I know their prayers played a big part in my recovery. My surgeon agreed.

"One thing in Dale's favor," Dr. Ballard wrote in his report, "was the strength of all the family members. It was amazing to me to walk down the hall to her room and see them gathered to watch over wife, mother, grandmother, neighbor, and friend. Quite an impressive crew."

Our feeling toward my surgeons was mutual.

Some through the Fire

God's Stubborn Love

God's gifts to me are beyond reckoning. He has bestowed them with a generous hand. They are the fruit (benefits) of the Spirit. Jesus is the Tree; we are the branches, and as the branches draw life from the trunk of the tree, so when we draw upon his strength, we produce rich fruit in our lives. God is good in his benefits. I know, for he has cushioned the hardest moments of my life and given me strength to go on. However hard the way has been, I am at peace. Forgetting that which is behind, I press forward to the mark of the high calling in Christ Jesus. I know I can trust him.

A history of popular hymns tells the story of George Matheson, a blind Scottish preacher who wrote that beautiful hymn "O Love That Will Not Let Me Go." He became blind at the age of eighteen, yet he went on to become a great preacher in the Church of Scotland. He was engaged to be married when his impending blindness was diagnosed. His fiancée changed her mind and broke their engagement. Realizing that George had great potential as a preacher, his sister studied Greek and Hebrew to help him research his sermons.

I marvel at the discipline and commitment of this hymn writer. William and Randy Petersen,

49

writing in *The One Year Book of Hymns,* tell in Pastor Matheson's own words how his song "O Love That Will Not Let Me Go" was composed in the Manse of Innellan, Scotland, on the evening of June 6, 1882: "'I was at the time alone,' wrote the minister. 'It was the day of my sister's marriage and the rest of the family were staying in Glasgow. Something happened to me, which was known only to myself and which caused the most severe mental suffering. This hymn was the quickest bit of work I ever did in my life. I had the impression of having it dictated to me from an inner voice, rather than working it myself.'"[1]

My book *Angel Unaware,* written in the mid-fifties, came to me in exactly the same way. I know how George Matheson must have felt as his hand obeyed his heart and his hymn was born.

In Perfect Peace

Although my Bible lay unopened on the nightstand in those dark days at Loma Linda, its words were engraved upon my heart through decades of study and prayer. God's promise to "keep him in perfect peace, whose mind is stayed on thee" came true. Our heavenly Father will not let us be tempted by misery beyond what we are able to bear.

When pain in my body was almost impossible to bear, the thought of the sacrifice God made in sending his only Son, Jesus, helped to ease my pain.

Proverbs 18:14 reminds us that "the spirit of a man will sustain him in sickness" (NKJV). The promise of Proverbs 17:22 also became true for me: "A merry heart doeth good like a medicine." It is amazing what a sense of humor will do for a person struggling to be well. Diane DuFresne, our niece, assisted Martha Brown in the early days of my recovery. Diane has a delightful sense of humor and kept me laughing to reduce tension. Her merry heart did me good like a medicine.

On one of my first excursions after my stroke, Martha and I ventured out to Los Angeles to be with my longtime friend Alice Van Springsteen, who doubled me at Republic Studios in the Roy Rogers westerns. Alice was being honored as the first female jockey by the Women's Referral Service, a prestigious organization for women who have excelled in a "man's world." My old friend is like the sister I never had.

Our motel room in the Red Lion Inn near the Los Angeles Airport was built to accommodate a wheelchair, so everything went smoothly as Martha tucked me into bed for a long night's sleep after the meeting.

At 2 A.M. I needed to go to the bathroom. As Martha helped me off my bed and I stood to my feet, she asked, "How do you feel?"

"Like Frankenstein," I replied.

We both laughed for a full ten minutes. When you are ill, depressed, and "stressed out," try thinking good thoughts that are pleasing to God. Expect a blessing. Christ has given us much to enjoy. If we trust in the Lord Jesus and lift him up in praise, he will gird us with his almighty hand and help us through our trials.

A stroke goes a long way toward eliminating false pride.

Rolling with the Lord

Life in a wheelchair never entered my mind for the first eighty-three years of my life. When I sang, "I'll never walk alone," I didn't think that someday I'd be *rolling* with Jesus on the path to Life City in a wheelchair.

In my chair I suddenly had time to enjoy things that I had been too busy to notice during most of my life. I'd been a take-charge kind of person. I would just go, go, go—too fast to smell the flowers or to notice many things God gave us to enjoy. Now I have time to learn what God wants me to learn.

Through long nights when I can't sleep, I have time to pray. I can see the moon outside my window and watch the sun come up each morning to warm the earth. All this is a glorious blessing once taken for granted.

I don't know what your handicap is, but remember: An affliction is an opportunity to learn the things we need to learn in order to enjoy the Lord of Glory. Think about that when things don't go right for you. Instead of grumbling, "Why did this happen to me?" just say, "Lord, whatever you have in mind, I want to learn. I want to be what you want me to be, and I want to learn from you. I want to appreciate you. I want to thank you by my attitude. And I want to thank you for all you've done for me by giving your life for me on the cross."

Don't let another day go by without allowing him to put joy into your life. I now see roses as the creation of God, I see beautiful trees as his handiwork, and I see God's hand in the storm, in quiet waters, and in each dawning of a new day. The first few verses of Psalm 103 contain the cry of my heart: "Bless the LORD, O my soul: and all that is within me, bless his holy name. Bless the LORD, O my soul, and forget not all his benefits: who forgiveth all thine iniquities; who healeth all thy diseases; who redeemeth thy life from destruction; who crowneth thee with lovingkindness and tender mercies; who satisfieth thy mouth with good things; so that thy youth is renewed like the eagle's."

When we people in wheelchairs are tempted to grumble about our infirmities and want the Lord to take us home to heaven, we must remember: We are under divine appointment. We are to think on the goodness and greatness of God and find purpose for our lives.

Helen Keller lost her ability to see and hear while still a baby. But even with these handicaps she was able to achieve an education and inspire thousands of people—especially those with handicaps. Of the darkness that inhabits the lives of the sightless she wrote,

Truly I have looked into the very heart of darkness, and refused to yield to its paralyzing influence, but in spirit I am one of those who walk the morning. What if all dark, discouraging moods of the human mind come across my way as thick as the dry leaves of autumn? Other feet have traveled that road before me, and I know the desert leads to God as surely as the green, refreshing fields and fruitful orchards. I, too, have been profoundly humiliated, and brought to realize my littleness amid the immensity of creation. The more I learn, the less I think I know, and the more I understand of my sense-experience, the more I perceive its shortcomings and its inadequacy as a basis of life. Sometimes the points of view of the optimist and the pessimist are placed before me so skillfully balanced that only by sheer force of spirit can I keep my hold upon a practical, livable philosophy of life. But I use my will, choose life and reject its opposite—nothingness.[2]

Bless Helen Keller. What an inspiration she is! She has said it all for me. I may never walk again. The thought brings me up short, but I must face it. My left leg might never again take the full weight of my body. But whatever happens, I can "walk" in my mind.

When your spirit needs to be raised, remember Philippians 4:8: "Finally, brethren, whatever things are true, whatever things are noble, whatever things are just, whatever things are pure, whatever things are lovely, whatever things are of good report, if there is any virtue and if there is anything praiseworthy—meditate on these things" (NKJV).

Things to Meditate On

Patience Is a Virtue

Patience is not a popular discipline today. We feel that the faster we go, the more we accomplish. It seems to be almost a virtue to say, "I'm so busy." We are determined to push everything at breakneck speed.

Roy and I have had a lot of animals during our lifetime. When we get a puppy, it seems like no time before he's grown. A cute little kitten becomes an independent cat in a few months. A baby, on the other hand, requires many years to reach maturity. Humans take much longer to grow up. God did not design us to be microwave men and women.

God's work is never hurried. James says, "Let patience have its perfect work" (1:4 NKJV).

We cannot teach the value of patience in the classroom or from the pulpit. I can write about its value, but my words will only be hollow. Patience is taught in our lives and by our actions.

Saint Francis of Assisi wrote, "No one will ever know the full depth of his capacity for patience and humility as long as nothing bothers him. It is only when times are troubled and difficult that he can see how much of either is in him."

As the phone interrupts my thoughts again (why don't I have the fortitude to let it ring?), I think, *Oh Lord, teach me to be patient. Right now!*

How to Have Friends

I have been privileged to have many friends, but each of us has just a few close friends. Usually the Lord provides them at just the times we need them most.

Charles Spurgeon was called "the prince of preachers." His grasp of the Scriptures and deep love for Christ infused his sermons and books, which are quoted in evangelical churches throughout the world. He wrote, "Friendship is the only thing in the world concerning the usefulness of which all mankind are agreed. Friendship seems as necessary an element of a comfortable existence in this world as fire and water, or even air itself. A man may drag along a miserable existence in proud solitary dignity, but his life is scarce life; it is nothing but an existence, the tree of life being stripped of the leaves of hope and the fruits of joy. He who would be happy here must have friends; and he who would be happy hereafter must above all things, find a friend in the world to come, in the person of God, the Father of His people."

Ralph Waldo Emerson said, "The only reward of virtue is virtue; the only way to have a friend is to be one." Good friends are good encouragers, but the greatest encouragement of all is in the Book: "Everything that was written in the past was written to teach us, so that through endurance and the encouragement of the Scriptures we might have hope" (Rom. 15:4 NIV).

Can We Get Along?

Every race has special and marvelous gifts. Why can't we look for those gifts and learn to appreciate them? Why do we fear each other so?

The Bible says, "He that feareth is not made perfect in love" (1 John 4:18) and, "If a man say, I love

God, and hateth his brother, he is a liar" (4:20). Love is not narrow, not restricted, certainly not racial! It is, as the song says, "a many-splendored thing."

Read the apostle Paul's definition of love in the thirteenth chapter of 1 Corinthians; just try to put that in a racial straitjacket! Jesus said that men would know us as his followers when "ye have love one to another" (John 13:35). Love is never a respecter of persons—nor of any particular color or race of people. The Bible calls upon us to love *even our enemies.* Is that possible? Have you ever honestly tried it? Have you ever tried to go the second mile, to bless those who curse you, to pray for those who persecute you?

When Jesus healed the ten lepers and only one thanked him for it, did he stop healing? No, he continued to heal for the glory of God—and not because he expected a word of thanks.

Let love, not appreciation, be your motive and you win.

God's Weathermen

When I listen to some of the talk shows in which nothing in a person's private life is sacred, when I read of children killing parents and parents molesting children, when I see the sleaze in the entertainment industry, I want to either scream or throw up. The forces of evil have pulled us so far down into the pit that only widespread repentance and spiritual awakening can lift us out.

Erwin Lutzer, a prominent theologian, said, "There is reason to believe that only a national revival can pull us out of the ditch into which we have slid. I am convinced—as all of us must be—that every human resource is now inadequate. Only the direct intervention of God can reverse our spiritual direction."

Revival, as I understand it, means the widespread renewal of the church. The church, however, cannot be revived until individuals are revived. Jesus told Nicodemus that "the wind blows where it wishes" (John 3:8 NKJV). We are not God's weathermen to discern where or how a revival may take place. But we can look at the past and see what some of the common denominators were in revivals.

Let it all begin with prayer meetings. From those will come a strengthening of this nation's values and valor, dedicated preachers and teachers, and prayer that starts in the home, spreads to the churches, and thence to the cities.

"If My people who are called by My name will humble themselves, and pray and seek My face, and turn from their wicked ways, then I will hear from heaven, and will forgive their sin and heal their land" (2 Chron. 7:14 NKJV). The daily news may depress us, but the good news is that God may yet restore America to spiritual health.

The Bible Has the Answers

My generation doesn't have all the answers—and neither does the Now generation. But the Bible has them—the inspired Word of God has *his* answers. It provides answers both for the establishment and for youth.

Speaking of the establishment, let's be clear that the young people of today are the establishment of tomorrow. That's why we should be sending them to the Bible now for the answers to the questions they are asking.

It begins in the home—in parent-and-child relationships. The Bible says, "Children, obey your parents. . . . Honor thy father and mother" (Eph. 6:1–2). "And, ye fathers, provoke not your children to wrath: but bring them up in the nurture and admonition of the Lord" (v. 4).

In other words, children are to love and obey their parents *for God.* Parents are to love, serve, instruct, and discipline their children *for God*—until their children are ready to move out on their own.

That's the way we did it with all our children. We did it, or tried to do it, the Christian way, and it has paid off handsomely. Every one of our children has found Christ—and all settle their problems the Christian way.

Take Up His Cross

Roy and I, along with the Sons of the Pioneers and Cliff Arquette, had signed for thirteen hour-long shows for ABC Television, the first of which was to be filmed in Seattle. Our closing number was "How Great Thou Art." Roy and I sang it standing under one of the beautiful arches of the Science Building, with great fleecy clouds as a backdrop.

Just before we started to do the first take on the number, Art Rush got a call from the powers-that-be at the network, ordering us to delete the word *Christ* from the third verse of the song. We refused, just as we had refused to take out the cross made of light thrown on the turf in Madison Square Garden when Roy sang "Peace in the Valley" some years before. The pressure was really put on us, but we were adamant about it. Later we learned that our refusal to delete the Lord's name was one of the factors that caused our show to be canceled at the first option.

What does Christ say about such things? He says, "Let him . . . take up his cross daily, and follow me" (Luke 9:23). He also says that those who follow him may be persecuted for their loyalty to him. Think of what he went through to give us eternal life. How paltry is a television contract in comparison with that? Christ said that with every temptation to waver in doing right, he would give us a way of escape. Though Roy and I have lost out more than once in secular work, we have never gone hungry. When one door has been slammed in our faces, another has always opened. We have found God completely honest in his promise: "I will never leave thee, nor forsake thee" (Heb. 13:5). He will be with us whatever happens. He has said so, and I believe him.

4

"This Will Hurt"

No chastening for the present seemeth to be joyous, but grievous: nevertheless afterward it yieldeth the peaceable fruit of righteousness.

Hebrews 12:11

The Greeks called strokes *apoplexy,* meaning "struck down." Of all the strokes Americans suffer, 15 percent are attacks from blood clots in the brain and 85 percent are from closed arteries. My problem was the latter.

As hard as the surgery was to endure, rehabilitation was even harder. People I considered to be my friends were suddenly asking me to endure incredible pain.

Over and over again I heard them say, "This will hurt, Dale, but it's for your own good."

For My Own Good

There were times when I thought my family and friends had turned against me. It seemed as though they wanted to make my recovery from surgery as painful as possible. My left shoulder and arm remained paralyzed for a long time.

One of the most excruciating exercises was the "gate test" at the Loma Linda University Medical Center. In this procedure I was asked to walk by holding on to parallel bars. After several tries I heard the therapist express disappointment in my inability to finish the course. The head of the rehabilitation department came in and looked over my records. He expressed surprise.

"Dale," he exclaimed, "you seem so young in spirit. I thought you were about ten years younger than you are!"

Before thinking I responded angrily, "So you think I'm too old at eighty-three to recover?" That unfortunate outburst brought on the only hard crying spell I had throughout the entire recovery period. That poor doctor. I'm sure he thought he was going to have an uncooperative patient on his hands. After my sobbing subsided, I took stock. I had not acted as a Christian. Strong crying, sharp words of criticism, and tears meant to my doctor that I was giving up, that I was not going to cooperate in my rehabilitation, that I would just remain in my wheelchair and pout. Worst of all, it showed that I had forgotten to trust the Lord.

Blessings that I so often took for granted were momentarily forgotten, yet my heavenly Father "daily loads [me] with benefits" (Ps. 68:19 NKJV). Stop and think about what is going on in our bodies and in the environment all around us:

- The faithful heart pumps enormous quantities of cleansed blood through a maze of blood vessels.
- The lungs silently take in fresh air eighteen to twenty times a minute.
- Our body temperature varies less than one degree.
- The orderly succession of day and night moves relentlessly on.
- The dependable seasons allow us to make our plans accordingly.
- The refreshment of sleep comes to renew us daily.
- The great variety of food satisfies our differing tastes.
- The delicate blossoms on fruit trees and flowering bushes garnish the earth.

- The birdsongs are orchestrated daily for our pleasure and for that of our heavenly Father.
- The simple delights of home surround us.

What riches God has given us to enjoy. "His compassions fail not. They are new every morning: great is thy faithfulness" (Lam. 3:22–23).

No Pain, No Gain

Early in my rehab sessions at Loma Linda, my therapists drilled me with memory exercises. I found them quite boring, even though I understood their function in restoring my ability to recall events in the past. My therapist would read to me a story, then question me on the details of the tale to determine how much my mind could retain. I suppose I did fairly well, especially if the piece read was interesting to me.

One day the therapists organized a wheelchair race in one of the hospital corridors. Since my left arm was paralyzed, I could hardly spin the left wheel on my chair, so there was no checkered flag flying when I crossed the finish line. By sundown that night I realized I would have to pay for my excesses. Excruciating pain settled into my lower back muscles, keeping me from sleep. I called for my electric heating pad and had it filled with water. Then I tucked it under my lower back and fell fast asleep. In the middle of the night I awoke in a purgatory of my own making. My heating pad had so scorched my back that it took a month of bandages and medications to heal it. But as my hospitalization wore on, I could feel once again the joy of the Lord upon awakening each morning, thankful that I had made it through another night. An "attitude of gratitude," the title of a sermon I had heard on the Trinity Broadcasting Network, given by John Jacobs of the Power Team, buoyed my spirit. With my heart in tune with the promises of God, I began to think like that little engine huffing and puffing toward the top of the mountain. I began to sing, "I can do it! I can reach the top and go home to my family."

When I was released from the hospital, my physicians arranged for me to take additional therapy at home and at St. Mary Regional Medical Center in Apple Valley. At one point our house looked like a YWCA. Eager young therapists worked me over with crusaders' zeal. When one would raise my left arm high, I would almost scream. Then I'd pray, "Lord, please give me strength." Each time he answered.

I made daily entries in my diary to recount my blessings: My eyesight was good (sharpened by earlier cataract removal and lens implants); I could hear; I could speak; my right hand could move to write; I could smell; I could taste; I could hear my loving family and converse with them. *Pretty good,* I thought, *for a speck of dust coming up on eighty-four years!*

My friend Vern Jackson at TBN often sings "I'm at Peace in the Potter's House." That's where I've been for half a century. The Master Potter, our Lord, knows just how much heat we can take as he fires us.

Three months to the day after my surgery, I was scheduled to give the invocation at the annual Golden Boot Awards in Los Angeles. This is the "Oscars" for western films and provides funds for the Motion Picture Home in Calabasas, California. Two days before the event, lower back pain became unbearable. I couldn't sleep, my eyes became lifeless, my face puffy, and my complexion devoid of any color.

In desperation my daughter Cheryl asked Dr. Isaeff if it would be all right to try acupuncture. One of his friends, a doctor specializing in endocrinology, had been able to measure some positive effects from acupuncture treatment. In any event, said Dr. Isaeff, "it couldn't hurt."

Cheryl went right to work. She scoured the entire Los Angeles area and settled on the office of Dr. John Chen, a highly recommended acupuncturist right in Apple Valley, our hometown.

Dr. Isaeff's three little words, "it couldn't hurt," set my recovery in a new direction and brought enormous relief.

5

On Pins and Needles

Beloved, I wish above all things that thou mayest prosper and be in health, even as thy soul prospereth.

3 John 2

On Friday, August 16, 1996, three months after my surgery, Cheryl and her husband, Larry Barnett, drove me to the small office of Dr. John T. Chen, Ph.D., O.M.D., located in a section of Apple Valley appropriately named Sunshine Village. Shooting pains in my neck and left arm were intense, I couldn't walk a step, and I had little appetite. As I was being wheeled into a new environment, I looked toward the east. Streaks of flaming red sky from God's coloring book rose above the dark blue mountains of Big Bear Lake. Not even pain and depression could keep my heart from praising God at the wondrous sight. I thought of my little friend Julie Wingate, who sings "God's Coloring Book," and of Dolly Parton, whose song "Red Sky in the Morning" has often turned my thoughts toward our loving Creator. Hope for relief from pain was kindled in my heart that morning.

A Godly Acupuncturist

Dr. Chen's gentle wife, Yifang, met us at the door of the clinic and showed us in. Dr. John, gowned in white and wearing a big smile, warmly welcomed us to the Mojave Holistic and Pain Clinic, "the integration of tradition and science." His credentials are: "Licensed Acupuncturist, Herbalist, Doctor of Oriental Medicine, and Instructor at South Baylo University." He told us he prays for all his patients and also, "I practice before God." Trained in Taiwan, Dr. Chen seemed to be well equipped.

He sat down with an assortment of tools, photographs, and diagrams to introduce us to the curious procedure of acupuncture that has brought health and healing to countless patients.

Dr. Chen began to massage my left shoulder slowly and gently, then my left arm, and then my left leg. Shortly after he inserted the needles, which are no thicker than a strand of hair on my head, they released endorphins—little nerve-helpers. It didn't take long to feel the more complete circulation of my blood, and with it came relief from pain, and inner healing. Amazing! My family told me that color returned to my face after that first visit and that puffiness disappeared from around my eyes within the space of half an hour.

Dr. Chen noticed that my left eye tended to droop. "The absence of blood," he explained and went on inserting needles in the proper places as he kept massaging gently my forehead above my left eye. The thin needles were pushed in so deftly, I hardly felt them.

Our medications today are derived mostly from herbs. It is curious that the Chinese have been successful for so many centuries in the science not only of herbs but also of acupuncture. The Bible says we are fearfully and wonderfully made, and that is dramatically illustrated by our bodies' response to the little pins of acupuncture.

Dr. Chen stresses the point that circulation of the blood throughout the body is vital to muscle tone. His procedures with needles and with gentle massaging have helped the blood in my spine (particularly my lower back) to circulate properly. I no longer awaken in the morning with pain in my back and in my neck, as I did before Dr. Chen's massages.

Medicine's "Miracle"

Acupuncture might be new to most Americans, but it is the oldest medical procedure available. Although more people have been treated with acupuncture than with all other modes of therapy combined, it is still called an experimental method in Western medical practice.

Most of the criticism of acupuncture is directed at the philosophical approach in which Chinese medicine is rooted. It's what we now call "holistic." The Chinese consider the mind, body, and spirit as one interactive whole with the environment. They believe that only by treating all of these elements as a single, balanced energy system can harmony and wellness be maintained.

Acupuncture addresses the body's energy force, which Chinese believe is running throughout the body along vertical pathways known as meridians. A person's health is influenced by this flow of energy. If the flow is insufficient, unbalanced, or blocked, illness can occur. Acupuncture releases chemicals into the muscles, spinal cord, and brain, triggering the release of other chemicals and hormones from the body that kill pain.

When news of my unusual treatment became known, other people came forth with testimonials about the value of acupuncture to deal with pain. A woman in Dr. Chen's office one day told me, "Dale, you have come to the right place." She also had suffered a stroke and now was walking and driving her car again.

If I had known about acupuncture four years earlier, I would have asked Dr. Chen for treatment during the painful hours of recuperation from heart surgery. Acupuncture is routinely used after a heart attack to help reopen clogged arteries by triggering the release of hormones that dilate blood vessels. Acupuncture can do the same for vessels feeding the brain. Another possibility, my doctor tells me, is that acupuncture may help surviving neurons to find new pathways, effectively bypassing damaged parts of the brain.

I am a prime example of someone who has been helped by acupuncture to regain health. In warm weather, I now enjoy sitting under the healing rays of sunshine here in the high desert of California, just as Dr. Chen prescribes. I sit with my back to the sun many mornings for at least ten minutes. In addition,

I struggle to get some exercise, although it's minimal compared with my activities of yesteryear.

My schedule is quite different today from what it has been for most of my life. I now have time to read, to pray, to talk with friends on the phone, and to scribble notes in my diary. But never far away are the memories of the missing ones—my beloved Roy, who died suddenly early on the morning of July 6, 1998, as I was writing this book, and our three precious children who have gone ahead, awaiting our arrival in heaven to be with the Lord forever.

6

Learning Humility

Except ye be converted, and become as little children,
ye shall not enter into the kingdom of heaven.

Matthew 18:3

On the east wall of our family room in Apple Valley, California, hang paintings of all our nine children. In the cozy corner where I sit in my wheelchair or lie on my cot for daily naps, I can survey my kids, who smile down on us as I pray for the six who are still living.

In 1949, two years after we were married, I became pregnant. The joy of the occasion was eclipsed by signs of trouble in the seventh month. My blood count showed that I was Rh negative. Roy was Rh positive.

My pediatrician told us that our baby might have difficulties because of our incompatible blood types.

Robin Elizabeth arrived shortly after midnight on August 26, 1950. Lying beside her glass-enclosed incubator, groggy from the ordeal, I gazed at my precious little gift from God.

"Is she all right?" I asked a nurse.

"She's okay," came a voice from behind me.

But she was not okay. God had let Robin arrive with Down's syndrome. If she had these irreversible characteristics and would need to live her life as a mongoloid child, well then, we would deal with it as a family.

At home I saw what my heart had feared: her little square hands full of the wrong creases, her tiny ears, her undeveloped bridge of the nose, her slanting eyes. It was hard to accept.

God knows, our pride was shattered when we had to present to our friends in the Hollywood community of the early 1950s a Down's syndrome baby, a less-than-perfect baby. In those days people saw such an offspring as evidence of genetic weakness in the parents. Mongoloid children were usually hidden because society was not willing to accept them. This was true even among Christian people in churches. But God also knew that if we would accept the challenge of caring for Robin, he could use us to witness of his love in new and exciting ways. Still, my emotions were torn between feeling sorrow for Roy and worrying whether I was adequate to care for our baby. Besides our own emotional lacerations, what would wee Robin herself be forced to experience throughout her life because of her physical disabilities?

The Angel of Death

There is a time and a season for everything, the Bible teaches. I gladly set aside pressing duties at the studio to care for my baby. At our first luncheon together, I was feeding Robin in our kitchen when she suddenly became fretful—restless, I think, because she missed Cau-Cau, Robin's name for her nurse, Claudia Jones. Suddenly she pushed her crackers and milk off the table. Tired and a little irritated, I tapped the tiny offending hand. Robin started to cry but suddenly turned off her tears, spun around quickly in her chair, and pointed to a picture of Jesus hanging on the wall behind her.

The action took my breath. I had no idea that my daughter had ever noticed the painting. As she pointed, I studied the picture carefully. There was the Lord, surrounded by a group of children of all races and colors. Robin seemed to be pointing out something to me that I had missed. Often after that incident, she would twist and turn until she had a full view of the painting. It was the most precious "sermon" she could preach.

Now dramatic events began to pick up speed. Robin began crying for hours nearly every night. Our household was already on edge because Cheryl, Linda, and Dusty were all fighting off the swelling and fever of an attack of mumps. We kept Robin away from the family, in an effort to spare her this disease. Eventually Robin refused all food but her milk and cried constantly. Despite our quarantine, she caught the mumps. A pediatrician came and gave her a shot, but still she grew steadily worse.

A gentle and gracious Christian physician responded to my call for help by examining my baby thoroughly. In his kindness for the retarded, he leveled with me. "Dale, the infection has gone to Robin's brain," he said. "She has encephalitis. I doubt that she will survive this. If she does, there will be severe brain damage."

I asked about open heart surgery to close up the congenital defect that had put a hole in Robin's heart. "No, don't do it," the doctor urged. "She would never survive the anesthetic. Keep her as comfortable as you can, and go on loving her. Learn all you can from the experience. That is what I would do if she were my child."

Near midnight, shortly after the doctor's visit, I was awakened by a spine-chilling howl and wailing coming from somewhere outside. I leaped from my bed, threw on a robe, and rushed outdoors to find Lana, our German weimaraner dog (Robin's special pet), watching intently the door of her room. Strange. I had heard of dogs wailing as death approached for someone they loved. "It's just a myth," Robin's nurse, Ruth, told me, trying to get my mind off the inevitable.

Robin's fever soared to a dangerous level. Her crying wrenched my heart. Ruth's explanation was that crying was her pain-reflex action from a headache. I settled into a bedside prayer vigil so Ruth could get a little rest.

At dawn a relief nurse named Virginia Peck took over; her assessment was that Robin had suffered a convulsion. She and Ruth put her in cool water and brought her out of it. We took turns walking her and bathing her face, carrying out the prescribed coffee enema for internal stimulation. But despite all our efforts Robin slipped into a semicoma. Our doctor came, looked at her, and shook his head. "There is nothing more to do," he said.

Late in the afternoon I remembered with a pang of self-reproach that my other children had not eaten lunch, so I hustled into the kitchen to fix something for them. They were all very quiet, sensing the approach of a momentous event in the little house out back, which had been built exclusively for our little angel to enjoy some privacy and to house her special medical equipment.

While standing at the sink, I heard distinctly, *I am going to take Robin.*

"All right, Lord. As you will," I said aloud.

When the food was on the table, I went to Robin's bedroom in time to hear an ominous rasping, rattling sound in her throat. The singing of a bird penetrated my consciousness as I sat there beside my darling daughter. Lana scratched wildly at the screen door in her last desperate attempt to get inside, yelping the same protective bark she used whenever she stood between Robin and a stranger. Ruth and Virginia shooed her away.

I stumbled outside for a breath of fresh air, seeking a place alone to pray. Roy took me for a walk. With tears streaming down my face, I begged God to take our daughter quickly and not to let her suffer anymore. When we returned, Virginia came outside and announced to us quietly, "She's gone." Never have I wept as hard, never as long.

In the Arms of Jesus

Family members were summoned; Roy signed the death certificate; a man from the Forest Lawn Mortuary took away her little body. Frances and Leonard

Photo courtesy of Russ Rohrer Photography

Photo courtesy of Russ Rohrer Photography

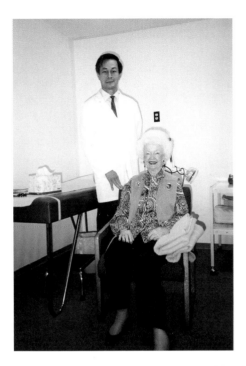

Dr. John Chen, Dale's
acupuncturist in Apple Valley

Joni Eareckson Tada with Dale at the Roy Rogers Museum in Victorville,
California, for the TV program *A Date with Dale,* aired by the Trinity
Broadcasting Network each Saturday morning

Longtime friend Ernie Worthington, at the 1996 Golden Boot awards in Los Angeles

Dale at the wedding reception of her grandson Dustin Roy Rogers and his wife, Julie, at the Apple Valley Country Club in California, June 1996

Homecare giver Martha Brown, wheeling Dale to the gravesite on July 13, 1998, for a visit

"The Cowboy's Prayer" on the wall around the Rogers' gravesite

Roy's grave, with Dale's beside his, at the family plot in Apple Valley

The bronze eagle at the gravesite

Their last photo together,
April 1998
Photo courtesy of Russ
Rohrer Photography

Eilers came to pray with us and offer comfort. Frances drove me around in her car for two hours while I cried it out and talked. Leonard stayed with Roy. When we returned, Robin's little house stood closed and dark. I could not bear to look at it. My baby girl would be buried on her second birthday, August 26, 1952.

The mortician put Robin in her tiny white christening dress, tied a blue ribbon in her hair, and placed atop her casket a photograph taken at her christening. On the way to the airport to pick up my brother, Hillman, Roy and I stopped at Forest Lawn to see that everything was ready. Roy asked me to go inside with him to look at our baby. I couldn't do it. I was certain I would break down and do something foolish, like try to pick her up. I just could not trust myself.

When he returned to the car, Roy had an expression of peace on his face. "That's the hardest thing I ever did," he said, "but I'm glad I did it. I feel at peace about her now. The minute I looked at her, I knew she was with the Lord. She looks like . . . like a small-size sleeping angel." He had selected a little child's blue casket. It looked so very tiny, he said, among all the flowers.

Part of me was buried that day in the mausoleum of that beautiful park. Robin's soul soared to be with

God, awaiting our soon-to-come reunion beyond the rainbow. I thought of Roy's words, "She looks like a small-size sleeping angel," and I pictured her reporting to the heavenly Father on her brief sojourn on earth. In *Angel Unaware* I wrote what I imagined our little baby said and how she must have concluded:

Well, that's it, Father. That's what happened Down There. That's how I delivered Your message, and I'm sure they got it. They learned, for one thing, that there are many mansions, or "rooms," in Your earthly house—that there's a room for the strong and a room for the sick, a room for the healthy and a room for the weak, a room for those born with ten talents, and a room for those with only one, a room for the rich and a room for the poor. A room for *everyone,* and something for them to do in that room for You. In Your house Down There are many rooms, where we study and teach and get ready to move into Your big light room Up Here.

We did pretty well in that room in my little house, Father. We taught them to see purpose in pain, and gave them messages on the crosses they have to carry around. You know, when Daddy sings now in his big rodeo show, he has a lot of big spotlights making a cross in the center of the arena. It's sort of a symbol of what's happened to him and to Mommy: the cross has become the great big thing in the middle of their lives. Everything else in their lives now sort of moves around it, like a wheel around a hub.

They're a lot stronger, since they got Our message. There's a new glory inside them and on everything all around them, and they've made up their minds to give it to everybody they meet. The sun's a lot brighter in Encino, since we stopped off there for a while.

And now, Father, please . . . could I just go out and try my wings?[3]

7

Learning Acceptance

Nevertheless not as I will, but as thou wilt.

Matthew 26:39

*I*n 1955 Roy and I were appearing at the Houston Fat Stock Show and rodeo when a letter arrived from Dr. Bob Pierce, founder of the humanitarian agency World Vision. As previously arranged, he was bringing to us a three-year-old Korean orphan made homeless by that dreadful war to be a part of our family.

Little In Ai Lee was chosen for adoption from among six hundred orphan "possibilities," and when we saw her coming down the ramp of an airliner in the arms of Dr. Pierce, it was love at first sight! Debbie (we had already renamed her) wore a Dutch bob and had soft brown eyes and a very solemn expression. We all wanted to keep her, so Dr. Bob went to work on clearing the way for Debbie's adoption.

Roy reached for her, and she nestled into his arms without a struggle. Newsmen followed us out of the airport to our car, snapping pictures, yet Debbie's expression never changed. With inscrutable eyes Debbie and our little Choctaw daughter, Dodie, looked each other over silently.

While driving down to Goldwyn Studios to report for work that afternoon, I held Debbie on my lap and tried to talk to her. I might as well have been addressing a lamppost. She knew a few words in English (Mama, Daddy, milk, sleep) but beyond that, nothing. When we reached the studio, I asked one of the older girls to sit in my dressing room with Debbie while she took a nap. One of the men brought Debbie a big, red balloon. She reached out for it, grabbed it, and held it close to her face with a grin as wide as the sky. Debbie, our Debbie, was home.

That night I tucked Debbie into bed next to Dodie and tried to teach our newcomer a short bedtime prayer. She smiled but didn't repeat after me. She couldn't yet. I turned out the light and left them with God.

Soon after Debbie arrived, we flew off to do a show at the Columbus (Ohio) State Fair, with all our children in tow. As we walked off the plane, the welcoming committee and a huge crowd of fans closed in around us and made such a racket that Debbie almost went into hysterics. She thought the bells and whistles and sirens signaled an air raid. The trauma of war still unnerved our daughter. She didn't calm down until we reached the hotel.

Debbie's Final Journey

Trouble, testing, triumph, and challenge characterized the events of 1964. The Religious Heritage of America chose me for its Churchwoman of the Year Award; I was invited to speak at the World's Fair in New York; Roy developed severe neck pains caused by three vertebrae that were jammed together because of worn discs; we took our children to Hawaii.

Debbie, now twelve, had blossomed into a beautiful young lady. After her birthday celebration on August 13, I took her to see Roy at a convalescent home in Bel Air, where he was recuperating from a neck operation. Debbie was all dressed up in clothes she had picked out herself. She was almost as tall as I was—exuberant, tireless, a frolicking filly who gave promise of tremendous energy and speed. I worried some about her easy familiarity with strangers, realizing with a pang that she would soon be leaving us.

Our daughter looked more like a young lady of eighteen than a twelve-year-old junior high school student. She loved to sit and talk with adults.

On the Sunday following her birthday, Debbie sang in our church choir. Her face was radiant—due in part to the fact that she would soon be on a bus with her friends from the church, heading to an orphanage in Tijuana, Mexico, where she would help to distribute a load of gifts to poor children. I think part of Debbie's radiance that day came from the joyful realization that she was becoming a young woman. Whatever the cause might have been, her face shone with pure rapture.

During the church service she caught my eye and nodded toward Dodie, who sat across the aisle from me. Dodie's face was as white as chalk; she looked over at me and whispered, "Mama, I'm sick." I took her out immediately. At home I told Debbie that plans would have to be changed; the bus trip to Mexico was off.

That stung. "Mom," she pleaded tearfully, "Kathy and Joanne Russell can't go if I don't go. Ple-e-ase?"

Eventually we relented. On Monday morning she and the Russell girls climbed into our church's bus, waved good-bye, and rumbled off.

I spent most of the day with Roy at the Bel Air Convalescent Home, where he showed encouraging signs of recovery from his neck surgery. As I drove home on the San Diego Freeway at about 3:30, I found myself deep in thought about our family—our health problems, the house, our growing children. Thank God I didn't turn on the car radio. If I had heard the news of what had happened near San Clemente, California, several hours' drive south, I would have lost my senses.

A Test of Faith

As I turned into the driveway at the ranch, I saw Ruth Miner ("Granny" to the children) looking at me strangely from the front porch. I parked the car and walked toward the house. A hot wind was blowing. As I entered the dining room, a few leaves blew in with me.

"Ruth," I exclaimed, "it's stifling in here! Why haven't you turned on the air conditioner?"

She walked over to me, took me gently by the arm, and led me into the living room. "Dale," she said softly, "you're going to have to get hold of yourself. Something has happened. The bus had an accident after it left San Diego. Debbie and Joanne Russell are with the Lord."

I stared at her. "With . . . the *Lord?*"

Then the news hit me like a hammer. Ruth was telling me that Debbie had been killed. "No! No! No!" I began to scream. "Not my baby . . . again!"

At that moment Dusty walked in from the chapel. Seeing my frantic state, he grabbed me and held me. "Mom!" he exclaimed, but I wouldn't stop. "Mom," he repeated, "get hold of yourself. As long as I can remember, you told me to trust Jesus. If you meant that, you'd better start trusting him right now. Debbie is okay. She's with him!"

I quieted down and took stock of the terrible situation. Had Roy heard? I hurried to the phone and called the hospital. Art Rush answered. He told me that the news media had promised not to release any news until Debbie's family had been informed. The news of our daughter's death sent Roy into such a tailspin that he had to be rushed back to the hospital at UCLA to be stabilized. Debbie had always been the one to meet him at the door with a kiss and a smile; she was the one who pulled off his boots, rubbed his aching neck, brought him coffee. She and Dodie often took turns combing Daddy's hair, trying different hairstyles while he watched TV. Later we learned that Debbie had asked her group for special prayer for her dad in the morning of the very day she died, because Roy was in the convalescent hospital, recovering from his surgery.

A strange thing happened on the day of Debbie's homegoing. In the middle of the night I was awakened by a loud, anguished moaning. I rushed to Ruth's room and found her wide awake. Together we went to investigate. Bowser, our dog, lay in a big chair in the living room. His head was hanging over the seat as he sobbed like a stricken mourner. We petted him for a while; then Ruth returned to bed and I went to the altar in our living room.

I lit the candles that night and looked down at the huge family Bible, which was open. My eyes fell on the words of Paul to the Hebrews, in chapter 12:

If ye endure chastening, God dealeth with you as with sons; for what son is he whom the father chasteneth not? But if ye be without chastisement, whereof all are partakers, then are ye bastards, and not sons. Furthermore we have had fathers of our flesh which corrected us, and we gave them reverence: shall we not much rather be in subjection unto the Father of spirits, and live? For they verily for a few days chastened us after their own pleasure; but he for our profit, that we might be partakers of his holiness. Now no chastening for the present seemeth to be joyous, but grievous: nevertheless afterward it yieldeth the peaceable fruit of righteousness unto them which are exercised thereby. Wherefore lift up the hands which hang down, and the feeble knees; and make straight paths for your feet, lest that which is lame be turned out of the way; but let it rather be healed.

Hebrews 12:7–13

I read aloud, "lest that which is lame be turned out of the way." I believe this passage refers to those who are watching professing Christians in times of deep trouble, people who might be attracted to the Way— watching to see if God's promises truly work in real life. If the Christian fails to demonstrate the power and grace of God in extremity, an unbeliever might be turned from the Way, thinking that God is not adequate to sustain us in the vicissitudes we are called upon to endure.

At Forest Lawn Memorial Park so soon again, I was surrounded by close friends—Art Rush, my friend Judy Whisenant, and Mrs. White, our pastor's wife, who would give the eulogy. Her husband, who had been on the bus when it smashed into an oncoming car, was still in an Oceanside hospital; Roy was still in the UCLA Medical Center.

Although I had steadfastly refused to look at the body of my precious Robin Elizabeth, I decided not to make the same mistake with Debbie. This time I went into the viewing room with the Russell family to look at my baby. There before me lay a pretty young girl asleep, dressed in the white dress she had worn at her sixth-grade commencement, garnished with a pink bow in her luxuriant black hair. Her long, slender fingers clasped the little blue stuffed animal she had won at Pacific Ocean Park on Saturday.

She appeared to be eighteen. My real Debbie was in eternity—*and in that moment I was with her, out of the body, in the Spirit.* There are no words to describe this experience; one has to go through it to understand it.

On my knees beside her coffin I thanked God for the nine years we had Debbie's love and companionship. I committed her into his hands. Then I got up and walked out of that place, and God walked with me. He had not left me desolate. He had come to me and taken my heartbreak into his own heart and given me freedom and joy.

8

Learning Release

This my son was dead, and is alive again.
Luke 15:24

In 1952 we finished an engagement at Madison Square Garden and had to play three other cities on our way back to California: Cincinnati, Ohio; Muncie, Indiana; and Owensboro, Kentucky. After that we planned to stop in Dallas to pick up Merry Little Doe, a baby girl who was a Choctaw Indian, just like Roy. We named our new daughter Dodie.

At first the director of Hope Cottage tried to discourage us from adopting Dodie. Seems that the law required Indian children to be adopted by Indian parents. But when Roy reminded the board of directors that he was part Choctaw, the problem was settled. Merry Little Doe would be ours.

In the huge stack of mail waiting for us in Cincinnati was a wire from a woman who ran a home for disadvantaged children, across the Ohio River from Cincinnati in Covington, Kentucky. She had a little girl in a wheelchair who wanted to see our show. We thought about Dusty, our only son, and all those sisters of his, so Roy asked if the woman had a little boy about five or six years old whom we could invite to the show.

The woman thought for a moment, then told us about a five-year-old chap in her care. "But I don't think you'd be interested in him," she added. "He's got a few problems." Roy told her, "Bring him along."

Harry John David Hardy, a tiny little fellow dressed in a yellow corduroy suit and a short-billed cap, arrived when we were onstage. When Roy walked up to him afterward, Harry stepped forward with his hand out. "Howdy, pardner!" he said, gripping Roy's hand with all the strength he could muster.

The little kid was in terrible shape. He had been abandoned three times before he was eight months old. He'd been either dropped on his face or beaten, and he had an unrepaired broken nose so disfigured he could hardly breathe. We took the woman's phone number and parted with a wave.

Roy and I discussed Harry's situation for several hours that night, wondering what life at home would be like if we took in a handicapped child. Finally Roy sighed and said, "Anybody can take in a perfect child. What happens to a little guy like this?"

Within twenty-four hours we had all the papers signed and had whisked this little fellow out of Kentucky and into our hearts forever. We named him Sandy. Roy often teased, "I've got one boy named Dusty and one named Sandy. If we ever get another one, we'll have to call him Filthy."

On the night we left on a bus with the cast of the show, Sandy had eaten so much dinner, he lost it all. In a hotel en route to Dallas, where we were to pick up Dodie, Sandy kept getting up and coming over to our bed to see if we were still there.

Back home in Encino, we took both Sandy and Dodie to our family doctor for checkups. Although Dodie was fine, Sandy was not. His head was enlarged, his bones were soft and pliable, and he had curvature of the spine—all caused by rickets and malnutrition. An electroencephalogram revealed a slight abnormality. His muscle tone was poor. Because his face had been smashed, he had almost no bridge to his nose.

As this poor little boy felt more at home in our house, he told us stories of earlier abuse. At a care facility he had been struck with a baseball bat for dropping a baby bottle. As tiny as he was, he was required to change baby diapers and feed other children. Whenever Sandy was "bad," he was made to sleep in a chair on the porch. Several times he woke up with snow all over him. During his growing-up years I often had to rock him to soothe his fears and calm him after a nightmare. He might have had a hard time sleeping occasionally, but the one thing Sandy could always count on was his appetite. He approached every meal as though it were his first and his last.

Private Rogers

Even before his teen years Sandy took an interest in the military. Every sailor, soldier, and marine he met—and he met a lot of them—became his idol. A burning desire to enlist for military service took hold of Sandy on a beach in Hawaii during our family vacation one year.

In January 1965 Sandy told us he wanted to enlist in the army. A year earlier he had begged us to give our consent for enlistment in the Vietnam conflict, which was heating up. We had refused then, wanting him to finish high school first. Now he was pressing us again for a chance to become a soldier.

"I want to serve my country," he said. "I want to prove I'm a man." I reminded him that he had not yet graduated from high school. "Mama," he said, "I promise you that I will get my high school diploma in the service."

Sandy was engaged to a lovely girl who attended chapel services with him. What about her? He said she had gladly promised to wait for him.

Our son's courage and determination were too much for us this time. We gave our consent. Off he went to Fort Polk in Louisiana to become a GI. I was present in the camp's chapel to see our son graduate at Polk, and on the parade grounds to watch him march in review with his company. I was proud of the way Sandy was fighting his handicaps so gallantly, proud of his love for the flag, proud of his passion to keep that flag flying.

With an eager heart Sandy volunteered to go to Vietnam but was turned down. "Your family has suffered enough," said a commanding officer who knew about the deaths of Robin and Debbie. So our Sandy was assigned to routine service in the tank corps and sent to a U.S. military base in Germany, "out of harm's way."

After Sandy went to Germany, shortly after Debbie's death, we moved to a new home in California's high desert at Apple Valley, where Roy had leased the Apple Valley Inn. The desert was good for me, with my bronchitis and bouts of pneumonia. I took to desert life with ease; the glorious sunrises and colorful sunsets were healing serendipities straight from heaven. We joined the Church of the Valley Presbyterian, where Dodie began taking instruction for membership. Dusty had a number of friends in nearby Victorville High School who attended the High Desert Baptist Church, so he joined that assembly. He was in his senior year of high school; Dodie was in the eighth grade.

Felled by a Bottle

Late in October I went to Texas to spend my fifty-fifth birthday with my mother. On October 31, 1967, the anniversary of my birth, I had a dream that shook me badly. I saw a rider on a horse galloping across a wide plain, heading straight for me. Suddenly the horse stumbled and fell. Rider and horse tumbled over and over in the sand. The horse got up but the man did not. He lay there motionless; I knew he was dead. I awoke sobbing.

On Monday I flew back to Los Angeles. Marion, a young lady we adopted at thirteen years of age in Great Britain during the 1954 Billy Graham crusade, was there to pick me up, as arranged, but so was Cheryl. There was an odd look on their faces. Without thinking, I blurted out, "Do we have a problem, kids?"

Cheryl was first to speak. "Sort of, Mom," she said.

Panic rose inside me. The dream! With growing fear and trembling emotions, I asked, "Who is it?"

"Mom," said Cheryl, "it's Sandy. He's gone."

Roy and Dusty came up as I stammered, "What do you mean, *gone?* Sandy isn't in Vietnam. He's in Gelhausen, Germany."

Dusty put his arm around me. "Mom, Sandy was at a party Saturday night, and some guys got him to drink a lot of hard liquor, and it killed him."

I almost fell to the floor. In an airport office, Cheryl gave me a tranquilizer as I struggled to make sense of what had happened. Sandy's body was to be flown home immediately after the military funeral in Germany, accompanied by an officer.

Once more we made the sad journey back to the Forest Lawn Memorial Park. This time we arranged for a military funeral. Sandy would be laid to rest in a crypt beside Robin and Debbie. Once more I stood beside the bier. There was my boy in his beloved uniform, the brave lad who had wanted so desperately to be a part of our country's action in Vietnam, a private first class felled not by a bullet but by a bottle! In my heart I raged in bitter denunciation of regulations that would allow an eighteen-year-old kid to be served enough liquor to kill him. Sorrowful and angry, I cried for this young man who had tried so desperately to measure up.

The officer who had brought Sandy's body all the way from Germany sat down with me and told me how it had happened. Sandy had worked hard on a three-week maneuver to earn his first-class stripe. He was overjoyed the day he got it but too tired for the wetting-down-of-the-stripes party in which his buddies participated. That sort of party was not appropriate for Sandy—he was no drinker—but this was tradition in the military, so he was coaxed into it.

To prove himself a man, Sandy drank with the rest. But that night he strangled on an overdose of liquor to which his body was not accustomed. Much as they disliked it, the officers in Sandy's unit were powerless to keep the soldiers from using their wiles to get liquor. Sandy was not the first victim of this sort of senseless celebration.

I remembered the last letter Sandy had written, telling us how grateful he was for the Christian home he had enjoyed, how he believed in God, in his country, and in his flag. He wrote of his eagerness to get to Vietnam eventually. It hurt me that he didn't make it, because he would have preferred death there to death by that bottle. After my outburst of anger I apologized to the officer and walked back to the coffin. I touched the hand of my son. "Thank you, Lord Jesus, that Sandy was a Christian." He had proven himself as a disciplined soldier, he had known the love of a wonderful girl whom he had planned to marry, and he had been spared future frustration and heartache in his struggle with his handicaps. I was proud of Harry John David Hardy Rogers, our Sandy. Having been rejected so often and having suffered such abuse from his natural parents, he had known in our family total acceptance, peace, happiness, and finally salvation by grace through faith in the Lord Jesus Christ.

Just before Christmas we received a small package from his commanding officer in Germany; it was Sandy's wedding and engagement ring, which he had purchased for his beloved Sharon. She arranged to have a cross made of them. Sandy would have liked that.

In the summer, Roy and I went to Vietnam for an entertainment tour under the sponsorship of the USO. In planes, jeeps, and barracks here and there I wrote a little book titled *Salute to Sandy,* signing over all royalties to Campus Crusade for Christ, International. The book was published on Sandy's birthday. Funds from its sale are still being given to Campus Crusade for its global evangelistic endeavors, so Sandy's testimony lives on.

Shortly after Roy and I celebrated our fiftieth wedding anniversary, Douglas E. Coe in Washington, D.C., a leader in the National Prayer Breakfast activities, sent us a warm letter of congratulations and inserted a poem titled "The Weaver" by Kristone. I cherish that poem, for it helps a believer to understand the reasons for the things that God brings into our lives.

9

Beyond Today

The just shall live by faith.
Romans 1:17 NKJV

A stroke curtails false pride. It reminds us we are temporal. Our life is "a vapor," the apostle James writes in his epistle, "that appears for a little time and then vanishes away" (4:14 NKJV). During my worst hours of depression after the stroke, I petulantly submitted my resignation from this earth. With my health gone and without strength to take care of myself, life in heaven with the Lord seemed preferable. The prospect of sitting in a wheelchair was not inviting. But I believe he still has things for me to do, and I'm willing to do them.

There is nothing to be gained by fighting the inevitable. I have learned that it's little use to pretend to be younger than you are or to wish for things you can never have. Since you can't change the date of your birth, you are not responsible for your age, only for what you make of the years God has given you.

My fellow senior citizens have done amazing things in the years of their seniority.

- At the age of 88 John Wesley was preaching daily with eloquent power and undiminished popularity.
- Benjamin Franklin invented bifocals at 78.
- Eamon de Valera was president of Ireland at 91.
- At 90 Pablo Picasso was producing drawings and engravings.
- At 89 Arthur Rubinstein gave one of his greatest recitals in New York's Carnegie Hall.
- Grandma Moses created her most famous work on Christmas Eve when she was 101.
- Albert Schweitzer built a hospital in Africa and managed it until he was 89.
- At 88 Michelangelo drafted architectural plans for the Church of Santa Maria degli Angeli.
- J. Irvin Overholtzer organized the global ministry of Child Evangelism Fellowship after he was 60.

- Johann Sebastian Bach composed some of his best music at 85.
- At 120 Moses' "eye was not dim, nor his natural force abated" (Deut. 34:7).

Sarah and Abraham started a family when they were well beyond childbearing years. When they were in their eighties, Joshua and Caleb led the Hebrew army across the Jordan to conquer the Promised Land.

How old are you? Thank God for every year of experience and press on. Need and struggle are what excite and inspire us. And that's true in retirement years as well.

A Judgment to Fear

My sedentary life allows my mind to review the indelible memories of momentous occasions in years gone by. One of them brings back a day in 1917 when I was five years old, sitting on the rolling green lawn outside the Baptist hospital in Dallas, Texas. My three-year-old brother, Hillman, was fighting for his life in the isolation ward. Hopeless patients were placed there so others would not be bothered by weeping relatives and gasping patients who were considered to be "on their way out."

As my mother and father sat weeping on the grass beside me, they pled with God to save my brother's life. Inside the hospital, mother had been unnerved by the screams of a dying man as he begged for someone to save him from the fires of hell. His screams could be heard throughout the isolation ward. Whether he found the Savior in time, I never found out.

Not many of the clergy preach on the fires of damnation these days. They prefer to dwell on the positive aspects of pleasantries here and of our glorious hereafter. But the Bible doesn't hedge. God's Word is quite explicit about the judgment of God when each person stands before the Creator to be judged. No, it is not a positive picture for those who have resisted the atonement freely offered to all who believe.

A Heaven to Gain

In Cleveland, Tennessee, one day I had a conversation with a heart surgeon after giving my Christian testimony at a concert of Christian musicians. The doctor told me about a patient of his whose heart had stopped. The suffering man had been resuscitated. During the ordeal he kept screaming for help because, he said, he was in hell. He begged for a preacher of the gospel to come and save his soul. A pastor nearby came to his bedside and showed the sufferer how to be redeemed and saved for all eternity.

The man responded eagerly. "Forgive me, Lord Jesus!" he cried. "Save my soul."

His physician was an agnostic, but when he saw his patient relax and noted the expression of peace on his face, the doctor gave up his agnosticism on the spot. With the dying man the physician humbly asked the Lord for salvation and was soundly converted.

Not everyone is as fortunate. An unbelieving woman told me one time, "Dale, your faith reads like a primer—too simple." I reminded her that Jesus taught that if we do not come to him in simple faith as a little child, we cannot enter the kingdom of heaven. Salvation is so simple that thousands miss it. Most people believe they have to earn it. Jesus paid the price with his life to redeem us. He would have taken that woman into the family of God, but as far as I can tell she died without acknowledging the Lord as Savior.

In the deep reaches of the night season, the destroyer whispers to me, "What about the years you wasted? Do you think he has wiped the slate clean?"

Quickly I respond, "Out! Out! My Lord paid for all my sins on the cross. I have nothing to fear from you!"

And then God's words calm my mind: "Peace, be still and know that I am God." It is then that he makes me to lie down in verdant pastures of rest; he leads me beside calm waters; my soul is restored. How I love him!

Those who look askance at my faith in Jesus are amazed that I can be happy despite all that has befallen me. I have much to be happy about. After all, I am a child of the King. He has been conforming me into what he wants me to be. I thank him for his correction. He anoints my head with his oil of gladness day by day. He has poured for me a very full cup of life; my joy runs over. Surely goodness and mercy shall follow me all the days of my life, and I shall dwell in the house of the Lord forever.

Answered Prayer at the Studio

Throughout my walk with the Lord, he has brought into my life many tests demanding both physical endurance and spiritual faith in moments of pressure. Any actor or musician who lacks composure or who crumbles under the pressure of deadlines and near disasters won't last long.

One of those times occurred near the end of a movie on which Roy and I were working with producer Jack Lacey. On the final day of shooting, the afternoon was far spent when Jack rushed up to me and said, "Dale, there's been a change in the script. We need you to write a song for our youngest actress to sing at the very end. And we need it in twenty minutes."

I went into my portable dressing room and got down on my knees. "Lord," I prayed, "you know I can't write a song in twenty minutes. Please help me!"

As I lifted my head, the words of the apostle Paul to the Corinthian believers popped into my head: "And now abideth faith, hope, charity, these three" (1 Cor. 13:13). There was something comforting about that exhortation, something sure, something full of hope. The words had a lilt to them. Would those sentiments help me to write a song?

I quickly found a tablet and a pen and began to scribble,

> Have faith, hope and charity,
> That's the way to live successfully.
> How do I know? The Bible tells me so.
> Do good to your enemies,
> And the blessed Lord you'll surely please.
> How do I know? The Bible tells me so.
> Don't worry 'bout tomorrow
> Just be real good today.
> The Lord is right beside you,
> He'll guide you all the way.
> Have faith, hope and charity,
> That's the way to live successfully.
> How do I know? The Bible tells me so.[4]

I read the words aloud, then jerked open my dressing room door and waved my notebook to Jack. On the double he brought in the girl who was to sing my song and end the shooting of the movie. Right there on the spot our musical director put a pleasant tune to my words. As the young actor gave it a try, others on the set wandered in to listen. Soon they were snapping their fingers and joining in. Jack decided to let all of us sing it for the movie. Since then the song has gone around the world and has been memorized by thousands—maybe millions—of people. I titled it "The Bible Tells Me So," and I still sing it occasionally on my TV program *A Date with Dale* on the Trinity Broadcasting Network.

Beyond the Sunset

Soon I will be leaving our six children and their spouses, our fourteen grandchildren, and our thirty-three great-grandchildren to join Roy in heaven.

My friend Vern Jackson, a singer on TBN, has written a song that I've taken as my testimony. Its title is "Here Today and Home Tomorrow." Some of the lyrics read:

> Here today, and Home tomorrow.
> I'll be free from the chains of flesh and bone.

I'll sail away from earthly sorrow
Here today and tomorrow I'll be Home.

The day of my departure is at hand. I base my future squarely on God's promise that "the foundation of God standeth sure, having this seal, The Lord knoweth them that are his. And, Let every one that nameth the name of Christ depart from iniquity" (2 Tim. 2:19).

God is bigger than any disability. Love him, appreciate his blessings, and trust him for the rest of the journey. He puts the rainbow at the end of the hardest trail.

If he can turn a disabling stroke into a stroke of hope, what can he do for you?

"Have faith, hope and charity, that's the way to live successfully."

10

The Coronation of the King of the Cowboys

November 5, 1911–July 6, 1998

O death, where is thy sting? O grave, where is thy victory?

1 Corinthians 15:55

*E*vening shadows were gathering over Apple Valley, California, on Sunday, July 5, 1998, as my husband and I sat together for a bite of dinner. I had eighty-six pages of this book written and was sorting information for more. Roy couldn't eat. I could see that he was struggling for breath worse than ever. Not far from my mind was the fact that exactly fourteen days earlier my husband's doctor had given him two weeks to live.

"Roy," I said, "Christ is in your heart, never to be separated. You need have no fear."

He told me he loved me and said he wanted only to rest. I took his hands in mine across the dining room table and asked the Lord to give my husband a restful night's sleep. Roy's caregiver came to help him to bed. How thankful I was that my recovery had taken me past my medical crisis so I could participate in the care of my husband.

As Nurse Joel wheeled him to bed that night, I heard my husband say, "Lord, please take me! I'm tired."

Once settled into bed for the night, Roy suddenly said to Joel, "It's been a long, hard ride. I'm dying, but I'm not going to heaven just yet. I'm going to wait for Dale." But our heavenly Father knew from the beginning of time the moment of Roy's departure for the portals of heaven, and that time was at hand.

At 4:15 A.M. Papa drew in his final breath of this world's air, closed his eyes, and departed for the Promised Land above. When Joel woke me and told me the news, I found it hard to believe, even though I knew Roy's death was imminent. I longed to join my husband on the happy trail to his heavenly coronation. Lying there in his bed, he looked like a young boy again. I looked at him until the mortician arrived. Death, the piteous exacter, had finally come, and suddenly I was robbed of my dearest friend on earth.

Through my tears I reviewed our nearly fifty-one years together. The movies we made, the trails we took, the supper clubs at which I sang with the big bands— all these are unimportant now. My real treasures are the children in our family circle, the friends we've made, the people who have come to faith in Jesus Christ the Lord through our testimonies.

A Nation Salutes

USA Today hailed my husband as "A hero in heaven." Our *Apple Valley Press Dispatch* headlined its loving salute "Until We Meet Again." *World* magazine wrote warmly of the "Good guy of a lost era." Columnist Michael J. McManus, in his "Ethics and Religion" feature on the day of Roy's funeral, paid tribute to his hero and remembered happy days of the fifties inside the Clover movie theater of Montgomery, Alabama, where he would watch movies starring his favorite movie star, Roy Rogers, and his band of noble riders. Writes Dr. McManus,

> Those cowboys were similar good guys in white hats who were always victorious over the bad guys, who looked evil (thanks to a four-day growth of beard).
> Roy Rogers was special to me because he operated on a higher plane of morality. For example, he

never shot first, and when he did shoot back, it was to shoot the gun out of the outlaw's hands, never to kill him. He saw women as people to be respected, not exploited. He loved animals, especially Trigger, of course, his golden palomino. . . . In short, he was a genuine hero.

A 1940s poll of children by *Life* magazine placed Roy Rogers in a three-way tie with President Franklin Roosevelt and Abraham Lincoln as the person they would most like to resemble. Why? He was a clean, moral person who fought for justice, but with a sunny disposition.

His movies were also fun. His sidekick, Gabby Hayes, was always funny. And even though Dale Evans, his wife, starred in many shows with him, they never did any of that mushy kissing stuff. But they did sing together, which seemed natural.

In his private life, Roy Rogers was a man of deep faith who made appearances with Billy Graham. I saw a recent interview with Roy and Dale Evans about how their marriage lasted 50 years. He said, "We don't believe in a 50–50 split of responsibility. We both put in 100 percent."

As I look back, his movies were important to me as a child because they taught me something about morality. My generation grew up knowing there is a difference between right and wrong. Within a few years of the demise of "The Roy Rogers Show" on television in 1957, Hollywood began teaching the young generation morally confusing messages about "anti-heroes"—likeable outlaws such as "Butch Cassidy and the Sundance Kid." More recently, a film like "Pulp Fiction" literally glamorizes psychopaths, people who kill without emotion.

We can see the ghastly result in children who walk into their schools with automatic weapons, killing fellow students and teachers for no reason.

William Bennett, in his introduction to *The Book of Virtues,* said its purpose is "to aid in the time-honored task of the moral education of the young." Moral education is "the training of heart and mind toward the good." Children are not born with a knowledge of such virtues as honesty, compassion, courage and perseverance. "If we want our children to possess the traits of character we most admire, we need to teach them," Bennett wrote.

Since Hollywood no longer is aiding in the moral education of our youth, parents and grandparents must seize the initiative to do so. How? First, we can discuss our own moral choices to do the right thing, though it requires effort and discipline. Another way of teaching virtue is by tapping a wealth of written material once taught to students to help them develop character. . . .

The earliest stories in such chapters as "Self-Discipline," "Compassion," "Friendship," and "Faith" are for the youngest children. The latter parts are more sophisticated, such as letters or talks by noted individuals. Consider "The Athenian Oath" that was taken by 17-year-old young men of Athens:

"We will never bring disgrace on this our City by an act of dishonesty or cowardice.

"We will fight for the ideals and Sacred things of the City. . . .

"We will revere and obey the City's laws. . . .

"We will strive increasingly to quicken the public's sense of civic duty.

"Thus in all these ways we will transmit this City, not only less, but greater and more beautiful than it was transmitted to us."

Each of us can be a Roy Rogers to young people by reading such material.[5]

An Obituary

Roy began life as Leonard Franklin Slye on November 5, 1911, in Cincinnati, Ohio—a bustling river town serving as a watery link from inland states through the Ohio River to the mighty Mississippi. His diminutive parents, Andrew and Mattie Slye, also had three daughters, so Roy got the heavy work around the house.

When he was seven the Slyes moved to nearby Portsmouth, where Andy worked in a shoe factory. Roy's father, an enterprising man, built a houseboat from pieces of a wrecked ship and moved his family into his craft to save rent and provide a bit of adventure for his children. The Slyes enjoyed their watery address for some years until a vicious storm poured so much water into the suburbs that Andy's floating castle drifted out of the bay into Portsmouth's city streets. He maneuvered the houseboat to an unoccupied lot in the town and anchored it to wait out the storm. Like Noah's Ark, the houseboat eventually came to rest on a vacant lot in Portsmouth, where it had, at last, an address.

Slightly built Andy, part Choctaw Indian, next bought a small farm outside of town called Duck Run. Roy's chores on the tiny farm included bagging rabbits in nearby hollers for the dinner table during lean times of the Depression. He and his father built a house on the farm—a house to make a couple of amateur builders proud. It had two stories, with a well out back and an outhouse to boot. Even though Andy Slye had Indian blood in his veins, tilling the soil was not one of his skills. He was nearly crippled permanently one day by the swift kick of an angry mule.

On the porch of this house Roy's three sisters and their dad would strum mandolins and guitars of an evening, making music all by themselves before the days of modern entertainment through radio and television. In the late 1920s Roy had saved up enough money to buy his own guitar and learned enough songs to entertain at square dances.

Roy learned to call dances like a pro at the schoolhouse on Saturday night. He could ride his horse Babe bareback at a gallop and swing under her neck. Roy often told of plowing behind Babe and hitting rocks and stumps that jerked the implement so drastically it would almost knock him down. One of the tests of a boy's grit in the early twenties was to run barefoot over the short, hard stubble of the school yard without flinching. It was always hard for Roy to be sympathetic toward modern youngsters who feel insulted if they have to walk a block to catch a school bus.

"The world doesn't owe anyone a living," Roy often reminded us.

Andy Slye had a bruising work schedule in a Cincinnati shoe factory. Because of the distance, he came home to his family only every couple of weeks so as not to miss any hours of work. Farming was not in the cards, so after being kicked by that mule, he began to look around for other employment. Roy also got work at the shoe factory with his dad to earn extra money.

California or Bust

One morning in 1931 at 4:30 A.M., as Andy and his son rose to go to work, Andy suggested to his son right out of the blue, "Leonard, let's move to California."

Roy was surprised. "You mean it, Dad?"

Andy patted his wallet. "I've got ninety bucks saved up. That will buy a lot of gas." Daughter Mary had been sending glowing reports of the Golden State from her home in Lawndale.

Mattie was talked into the venture, and soon Roy and his parents were rolling westward on Route 66 in a 1923 Dodge touring car. For two weeks they chugged along, eating stored grub, sleeping under the stars, and dreaming of decent wages in California during the terrible depression. With only two years of high school under his belt, Roy could hope for little more than manual labor.

One of his first jobs was picking peaches all summer in the San Joaquin Valley at Tulare. The temperature often reached one hundred degrees in the shade, and there seemed to be no end of ripening fruit that had to be picked quickly. Roy would mop his brow and squint at the sun, thinking, *There's got to be a better way to make a living.*

I can just see Roy under a peach tree at night, picking his guitar and singing,

I get some slickum on my hair
and put on my Sunday pants,

My pay in my pocket now I'm headin' for the
   dance.
There's a pretty gal a-waitin' there I'm hopin' to
   win,
I'm just a buck-eyed cowboy
from O-H-i-o-o-o.

Back in Los Angeles a fellow named Ed Boice
heard Roy sing and strum a guitar and invited him
to try out with the Rocky Mountaineers. This asso-
ciation marked the start of Roy's career in music. The
boys lived on chipped beef and gravy as they traveled about, and were glad to get that! Soon Roy
joined another group, the International Cowboys.

The following year he organized a gaggle of guitar strummers and singers and called his group the
Pioneers. A radio announcer thought the boys looked
awfully young for such a man-sized title, so he introduced them as the Sons of the Pioneers.

The name stuck and is used to this day.

The young troubadours took a barnstorming trip
through Arizona, New Mexico, and Texas in 1933.
They lived off jackrabbits and anything they could find
to eat. In a little radio station at Roswell, New Mexico, the boys listed on the air the things they loved to
eat. Roy told his audience that his passion was lemon
pie. A note arrived at the station that afternoon, prom-
ising that if Roy would do his Swiss yodel, he would

receive a lemon pie that night. He gladly obliged, and sure enough, a tall young woman appeared at the door of the radio station with two lemon pies just for him. She was Grace Arline Wilkins and Roy was smitten. A year later she became Mrs. Roy Rogers.

The Big Break

Two incidents in two days set Roy Rogers on a course of international success. The first occurred in Glendale, California. Roy was sitting in a salon, waiting for his hat to be cleaned for an engagement with the Sons of the Pioneers, when a man in a big hurry bolted through the front door.

"What's the excitement?" Roy asked.

"I gotta have a cowboy hat," the man gasped. "Can I get one in here?"

"I suppose so," Roy replied. "What's it for?"

"Well, I've got a screen test in the morning, and I've got to be wearing a cowboy hat."

"Where ya headed?"

"Republic Studios. They're lookin' for a singin' cowboy," the man explained.

Roy thought, *A singing cowboy? Maybe I'll mosey on out there to see what's going on.* He had no agent, only pluck. But as Roy was fond of saying, "I must have been where God wanted me to be."

Just as he expected, the studio was jammed with people. Roy opened the gate and started to enter, but a guard stopped him. "You can't get in here without a pass," he was told.

Roy waited an hour or two. Finally, after the lunch hour was over, a big group of extras flowed back through the gates to resume their duties. Roy stayed on the opposite side of where the guard stood, and sneaked in unnoticed with the crowd.

Inside, he was trying to decide where to go when a hand came down on his shoulder. *Oh, no!* he thought. *They're going to throw me out.* He turned around to see the smiling face of Sol Siegel, the producer. "Hello, Roy," Sol began. "What are you doing here?"

"I heard you were looking for a singing cowboy," Roy explained, "and since I've been singing with the Sons of the Pioneers, I thought maybe I'd try out."

"Well," said the producer, scratching his whiskers, "we have about seventeen fellows applying, but we'll see what we can do."

Now, who takes charge of things like that? God does. Nothing happens by chance in the economy of God. My husband's rise to his status as King of the Cowboys has the fingerprint of providence all over it. I shared in those exciting times with Roy, but for much of the drama I just got a good grip and hung on! I agree with country star Randy Travis, who said of Roy, "There are no people doing movies today who are the kind of example Roy was to the kids."

Well, as a lot of people know, Roy was inked by Republic Studios in 1938 to a contract for the movie *Under Western Stars.* He had bit parts in that movie and sang with his buddies "Tumbling Tumbleweeds" and other songs made popular by the Sons of the Pioneers.

Away from Republic Studios Roy sang, "Don't Fence Me In" in 1944's *Hollywood Canteen.* He also showed up in the 1948 musical revue *Melody Time.*

He always made it clear to interviewers that he only played himself in movies. "I'm an introvert," he'd say. "I never considered myself an actor. I'd look at a scene and ask, 'How would Roy Rogers do it?' and I'd try to do it that way."

My husband was voted the top western star by theater owners from 1943 well into the 1950s. This kind of popularity took us to rodeos in such places as Madison Square Garden and lots of state fairs. When not wearing fringes, Roy preferred flower-printed shirts and snug pants.

Roy's movies were always morally clean. As a boy, Roy was taught by his parents that hitting below the belt was a cowardly thing. "I don't believe that kind of thing is entertainment," Roy often said, "no matter how you look at it."

Happy Trails

We often sang together in appearances around the country, as well as in our movies. One of our most popular songs was "Happy Trails," which I wrote shortly after we were married in 1947. "Happy trails" had been Roy's favorite phrase when signing autographs, so putting a musical score to it and adding some additional verses seemed a natural thing to do.

For the melody, I recalled a phenomenon at the Grand Canyon, on the donkey trail from the rim to the river below. As the guide started down the steep path with his donkey and a group of hikers, he would yodel a deep note followed by a high one. Far below at the camp a guide would answer back with the opposite call, starting with the high note and ending with the low one. At the top came "Da Da De-e-e-e-e." And at the bottom came the answer with the opposite intonation: "De-e-e-e Da."

The call became a repeated refrain for my lyrics.

Happy trails to you,
Until we meet again.
Happy trails to you,
Keep smiling until then.
Who cares about the clouds
If we're together?
Just sing a song and bring

The sunny weather.
Happy Trails to you,
'Til we meet again.

"Happy Trails" seemed to fit perfectly as a salute to our friends, as the name of our foundation for children's aid, as our sign-off on television programs, and often as a greeting for fans.

Roy and I would often sing other verses of the song together, including the following:

Happy trails to you,
It's been great to say hello.
And to share with you
The joy we've come to know.
It started on the day that we met Jesus.
When He comes into your heart
He really frees us.
For a life that's true,
Happy trails to you.

In June 1965, after Sandy died while serving with the U.S. Army in Germany, and after Debbie was killed in the bus accident on the San Diego Freeway near San Clemente, we moved to the sleepy little town of Apple Valley near Big Bear Lake north of San Bernardino, California. Here fast friendships were forged; nearby in Victorville the Roy Rogers and

Dale Evans Museum was established; and here we've enjoyed the constant flow of visitors from all over the world.

Until We Meet Again

The day we knew would come but never really expected to see dawned bright and clear on July 6, 1998. The high desert sought to bring cheer with pink-orange colors as I struggled to accept my loss.

On Saturday, July 11, family and friends gathered to lay my beloved to rest. Flowers filled our house and graced the museum's various rooms. Some respectful friends simply came and stood outside to pray. A noon service was planned for the public at our sanctuary of the Church of the Valley Presbyterian in Apple Valley; another service was convened for family and close friends at 5:30.

Actors, singers, musicians, politicians, and just plain folk by the thousands gathered with a police and military honor guard to pay tribute to Roy. A solid phalanx of bright red carnations (the state flower of Ohio) covered my husband's casket. The current members of the Sons of the Pioneers sang at the service; Pastor O. William Hansen led the prayer of confession and gave the assurance of pardon through the death of Jesus Christ on the cross. Pastor Hansen's sermon followed the majestic hymn "How Great Thou Art" and other songs, ending with the creed from the Book of Common Worship: "This is the good news which we received, in which we stand, and by which we are saved; that Christ died for our sins according to the Scriptures, that He was buried, that He was raised on the third day; and that He appeared to Peter, then to the Twelve, and to many faithful witnesses. We believe He is the Christ, the Son of the Living God. He is the First and the Last, the Beginning and the End. He is our Lord and our God . . . Amen."

Our pastor presented Jesus as the ultimate trail, because he is the way that leads to God. In his meditation at Roy's memorial service Pastor Hansen spoke of the many trails that constituted Roy's life.

> Roy walked many trails. All of us are here because he was transparent and because he allowed us to walk those trails with him.
>
> There was the *Glory Trail* that led through his early years out of struggle into incredible fame and success in later years. The Glory Trail led from the simple days of Leonard Slye of Duck Run, Ohio, to the stellar days of the King of the Cowboys in Hollywood.
>
> And then there was the *Trail of Tears.* On that trail the beautiful family portrait became stained with

tears—the death of lovely Robin shortly after her birth, the death of Debbie in a tragic accident, and then of Sandy in the military in Germany. There was the loss of Mattie and Pop and Mary and Betty Sue, and sisters Cleda and Kathy, and a myriad of blows that rained down along the way on the Trail of Tears.

And then there was a third trail—the *Trail of Jesus*. Roy made the decision to receive Jesus as his personal Lord and Savior. The Glory Trail, the Trail of Tears, and the Trail of Jesus. Roy walked all three. And now at this time of his death, having achieved the age of eighty-six years, Roy has come not to the end of the trail but *to the trailhead of life's greatest adventure.*

If it weren't for the Glory Trail that Roy walked, you and I would not be here today. It is the fond memories of that trail that Roy allowed us to walk with him that draw us all together.

Throughout his life Roy never lost his grip on who he was. As Dale puts it, "Roy's personal credo was, 'I am what I am . . . and that's all I am.'" He honored the rich heritage of his roots, the quixotic adventures growing up on a houseboat on the Ohio River, the carefree life on the farm at Duck Run, the odyssey of his family in the 1923 Dodge traveling across country on Highway 66 into California, the poverty and struggle, and the good family and warmth of music that would last a lifetime, to be valued above everything else.

One thing more that Roy has taught his family is the last crucial lesson—the lesson on how to die. These last weeks and months were not easy. At times they were very difficult. But when the time came to die, Roy faced it well. There were moments left for the familiar crinkle in his eyes and the impish smile and the whisper of his own trusting prayers. He did not lose his grip on faith, for faith is really the grip of God's hand clinging in love to ours.

On the Glory Trail Roy kept a grip on his own personal reality.

On the Trail of Tears he kept a grip on his own sense of integrity.

On the Trail of Jesus Roy kept a grip on his own personal faith through God's own grip of eternal grace upon Roy's heart.

The Trail of Jesus leads to his cross, where Jesus laid down his perfect life in the place of our broken and sinful lives. In his dying on the cross, Jesus exchanged places with you and me. He suffered the consequences of our sins. He took our place and gave us his place, that by faith and only by faith in him, accepting him as Lord and Savior, he bestows upon you and me his priceless gift. The gift of his forgiveness and love is a pure gift, never to be withdrawn. It's a gift neither earned nor deserved—a gift that lasts and lasts as the Trail of Jesus leads beyond the cross to eternal life. And it can be the gift of abundant and eternal life for you as it has surely proved to be for Roy, if you receive Jesus as your Lord and Savior *today.*

From the Mouths of Children

Children know their parents as no others do. Here is what our kids have to say about their papa.

My firstborn son, Tom, wrote, "I never knew my real dad. So for the first twenty years of my life a dad image was missing in my life. When Roy came into my life, I found a man who became a real father to me—finally! He was a man who revered fairness and honesty, a man of his word who could be depended upon. He really knew what commitment was and he practiced it. He was a down-home guy who became an international model for right living. His legacy has become invaluable for people all over the world. I miss him. He loved me and I loved him!"

Cheryl recalls her father's empathy with children and with animals. She remembers his uncommon skill with horses in the "Liberty" act at state fairs, when the steeds performed for him free and unharnessed. She also remembers a short-lived venture to raise rabbits on their ranch in the San Fernando Valley. "Dad's only failure with animals," Cheryl said, "was his failure to control the rabbits, who multiplied more quickly than he could give them away—

until that fateful day when they sealed their own fate by multiplying to the number five hundred."

Linda remembers her papa as "an awesome hero. He was a wonderful man, a very special father. He loved his family and provided for their needs while teaching his children the value of a dollar and the importance of working hard and never expecting to get something for nothing.

"As children, we shared our papa with kids in every country around the world. He could walk into a hospital ward, and the faces of those kids would light up with a new hope and a determination to get well.

"We shared our papa with studios, movie theaters, state fairs, rodeos, recording sessions, radio programs, location sites, and all kinds of public appearances. His fans adored him, and the lessons he taught onstage or at the microphone were the lessons he taught us at home—lessons on honesty, truthfulness, being fair, equality for everyone, responsibility, and never making fun of anyone who was different.

"We shared our papa with the world all of our lives, and in death we are sharing him again. But we cannot forget that God shared him first with us. He loaned us this awesome hero, this wonderful man, and this very special father for eighty-six years. And we are very grateful for the time that we had with him."

Dusty noted that Roy Rogers was a star because of his childlike spirit. "And Dad did not like late!" he observed. "Dad loved to be where he was and he loved to do what he did."

Marion, at age thirteen, had never known the love of a father or a mother. Without the care of Roy and Dale, she said, and their guiding and modeling for her, "I would never have known how to be a parent to my own children."

Dodie expressed her thoughts this way: "A dad changes throughout your life. When I was a little girl, he was my daddy, who hugged me and played with me; as I was growing up, he was a steadfast pillar— gentle and kindhearted but strong. He was consistent in discipline, and I always knew the boundaries. (Mom I could sometimes bend.) He led by example, by trusting, by honesty, and even by working on his weaknesses, which helped me to get through mine. He was a dad I was proud of, a man respected among all men."

The Trail Ahead

As I reflect on my life with my beloved Roy for almost fifty-one years, I am deeply grateful to God for those years, and for the large family he has allowed us to raise.

When I invited the Lord Jesus Christ into my heart and life in January 1948, I implored him, "Lord, cleanse me from all sin with your precious blood, make me a new creature in you, and as your child, use me in any way you choose. Whatever it takes, Lord, I want to be your child; temper me in your spirit. You are the Potter; I am the clay." I have been on the Potter's wheel ever since that day in the winter of 1948 because the blessed Potter took me at my invitation. I know that I am his child, and he knows how hot the fire must be to set me for his use. As my good friend Vern Jackson sings, "I am at peace in the Potter's house today."

Pastor Hansen appealed to his audience to enter Roy's "great adventure" by making Jesus Christ Savior and Lord: "Roy said those words. He believed in Jesus and followed him. That fact makes this day a celebration of Roy's own resurrection. He himself has completed this leg of his journey, and it has been an exceptional adventure. But let me assure you that it is nothing to compare with the extraordinary adventure just ahead."

Roy wanted to be buried at sunset, and we were able to grant his wish. Our burial sites had been purchased in a small interment park located on the slope of a mountain east of Apple Valley, called Sunset Hills Memorial Park. Our burial plots are located inside a low wall circling a grassy area. Granite plaques mounted on the wall quote Psalm 121 under the heading "A Psalm for Dale," and under the heading "A Cowboy's Prayer" for Roy is engraved, "Oh Lord, I reckon I'm not much just by myself. I fail to do a lot of things I ought to do. But Lord, when trails are steep and passes high, help me to ride it straight through. And when in the falling dusk I get the final call, I do not care how many flowers they send. Above all else, the happiest trail would be for You to say to me, 'Let's ride, my friend.'"

As water cascades down from a huge mountain of rock in the background and spreads into a pond beside the graves, a bronze eagle seizes a fish from the water and prepares to soar above the granite inscription of Isaiah 40:31: "But they that wait upon the Lord shall renew their strength; they shall mount up with wings as eagles; they shall run and not be weary; and they shall walk, and not faint."

Roy's casket was placed in a black, glass-sided carriage provided by Chet Hitt, owner of the cemetery. The somber rig and its burden were pulled by a black Clydesdale the last half mile of the journey. At the head of the procession was a lone bagpiper followed by the Single Action Shooters Society cowboys in black outfits complete with spurs and black armbands.

The hearse was preceded by volunteers from the San Bernardino County Sheriff's Posse on horseback.

Our grandsons followed behind, outfitted in white shirts and black pants.

Pastor Hansen read from the Psalms after the casket was in place at the grave site. All of our children, grandchildren, and great-grandchildren gathered around to hear our pastor's words of comfort and hope. I prayed as a singer with an acoustic guitar played and sang "Amazing Grace."

"You can feel the presence of Christ in this magnificent setting," Pastor Hansen said, as a flock of doves circled the crowd and then streaked toward the setting sun. The jingle of the spurs on the men who filed by the casket and the snorting of the horses of the posse brought back memories of the world we enjoyed for so long. I don't think there were many dry eyes in the group as we stood to say good-bye to a wonderful man. On the slow journey back to our house I heard Roy singing,

> Last night as I lay on the prairie
> And gazed at the stars in the sky,
> I wondered if ever a cowboy
> Could drift to that sweet by and by.
> They say there will be a Great Roundup,
> And cowboys like doggies will stand
> To be marked by the Writer of Judgment,
> The Creator who knows every brand.

Yes, with my husband I found the rainbow on many a hard trail. Now my path is growing steeper, but I see the bow in the cloud, a token of God's mercy and grace for me, for you, and for all whose trust is in the Savior. Death for the believing Christian is the ultimate stroke of hope.

Notes

1. Robert K. Brown, et al, eds., *The One Year Book of Hymns* (Wheaton: Tyndale, 1995), March 8 entry.
2. *Breakfast with God*, drawn from original manuscript by W. B. Freeman Concepts, Inc. (Tulsa: Honor Books, 1998), 72.
3. Dale Evans Rogers, *Angel Unaware* (Grand Rapids: Revell, 1953), 63.
4. Dale Evans Rogers, "The Bible Tells Me So." Copyright © 1955 by Paramount Roy Rogers Music Co., Inc. Copyright renewed 1983 and assigned to Paramount Roy Rogers Music Co., Inc. Used by permission.
5. Michael J. McManus, "Ethics and Religion," *Intelligences Journal and New Era,* 11 July 1998. Used by permission.